MANNERS
Made Easy

FOR TEENS

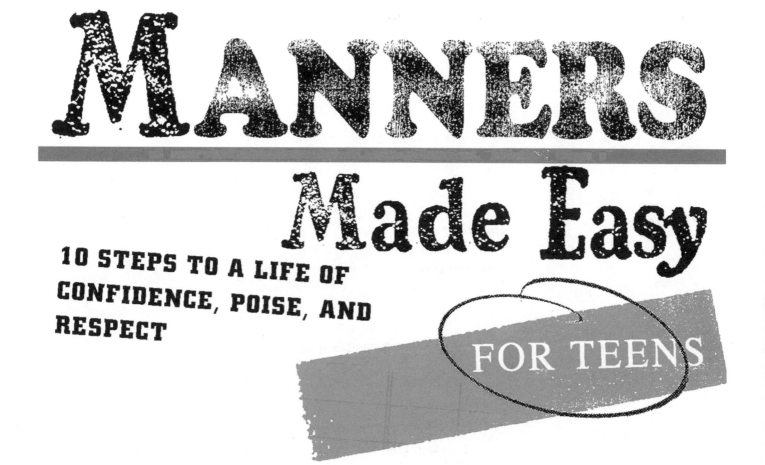

MANNERS
Made Easy

10 STEPS TO A LIFE OF CONFIDENCE, POISE, AND RESPECT

FOR TEENS

JUNE HINES MOORE

B&H
PUBLISHING GROUP

Nashville, Tennessee

ISBN: 978-0-8054-4459-9

Published by B&H Publishing Group
Nashville, Tennessee

Dewey Decimal: 395
Subject Heading: COURTESY \ ETIQUETTE

1 2 3 4 5 6 7 8 9 10   10 09 08 07

The author would like to thank the following people for their invaluable help in creating *Manners Made Easy for Teens*: David Webb, executive editor; Kim Overcash, managing editor; Diana Lawrence, illustrator; Matt Stewart; Stephanie Huffman; Zan Tyler; Beverly Wait, homeschooling mom; Bucky Rosenbaum; and Tim Joiner.

To contact the author, you may e-mail her at mooremanners@sbcglobal.net or call her at 501-224-1333.

TABLE OF CONTENTS

Student Pages

MAXIM:
Etiquette rules are in our heads; manners are in our hearts. Together they keep us from embarrassing others or ourselves.

HOW TO USE THIS BOOK

Dear Reader,

You may be the most well-mannered teen in your community, or you may see no conceivable reason to learn a bunch of rules your great-grandparents thought were important. Either way, this workbook can be fun and extremely useful to you. In these pages you will find helpful advice that can make a difference in your life right now and in the years to come.

Manners were God's idea, and He kept it very simple for us. All manners are based on the Golden Rule, which basically says, "Do for others what you would like them to do for you." Even the *Wall Street Journal* quotes that rule as the basis for all business and social interaction. This simple rule allows us to put other people at ease, feel good about ourselves and what we do, and leave awkwardness and fear behind.

Now, you may come from a home where good manners and the Golden Rule are taught and practiced daily, but your parents know that our society seems to have forgotten the need for proper manners, etiquette, and decorum. Relationships have been irreparably damaged, and many promotions in business and even jobs have been lost as a result.

It doesn't have to be this way.

Etiquette is really nothing more than a code of proper behavior that greases the squeaks in our contact with people. Knowing the basic rules of etiquette will provide you with the tools you need to:

- impress college admissions officers

- succeed in a job interview

- obtain the admiration of the opposite sex

- earn compliments, respect, and recognition

- turn self-consciousness into self-confidence

Of course, it's one thing to read a book about making small talk in an awkward situation, going on your first job interview, or what to do when your cell phone rings in church. It's quite another thing to live through the experience. Making a *faux pas* (a French phrase meaning *mistake*) while we are eating at home with the family may not be terribly painful, but what about when we make an embarrassing mistake while dining with a friend's family or while on a date?

If you fear doing or saying the wrong thing, it's simply because you don't know the rules. With the training you receive in this manual, you will have every reason to be more confident and less self-conscious in public. Everyone has social skills, good or bad, but you will know the rules and how to put them into practice. You will learn how to focus on others and not so much on yourself. New doors of opportunity, success, and enjoyment will open up for you, and wisdom you gain here will serve you all the days of your life.

You can read this book on your own, but ideally you will work with a parent or teacher to learn and practice the skills taught herein. Each lesson includes at least one exercise or role-playing scenario that will help you turn a simple list of rules into life-changing habits. Have fun while learning and practicing these rules: They are your friends.

Think of it this way. You wouldn't risk ridicule and injury by playing an organized sport without knowing the rules or having the proper equipment. And you would not think of performing in a stage play before a large audience without knowing your lines or having some training in the theater. No matter what you choose to do with your life, there will be many crucial moments when you find yourself in the spotlight, when it seems that everyone is suddenly watching everything you say and do. Will you shine or stumble? If you will practice and prepare for these moments, etiquette can make the difference.

Remember, as you participate in the exercises in this book, do not correct the etiquette of others. Correcting other people's manners is rude and only embarrasses them. Only critique another's manners if that person or your teacher asks you to make suggestions.

With the rules of etiquette in your head and the Golden Rule in your heart, you will not embarrass yourself or others. With new confidence in your social skills, you can focus on getting to really know people and experiencing good times together. You won't have to be self-conscious, living in constant fear of making a mistake or saying the wrong thing and being ridiculed for it.

As the author, I pray God's blessing on your efforts to "grow in wisdom and stature, and in favor with God and man" (Luke 2:52).

Enjoy!

June Hines Moore

LESSON 1

MAKING A GOOD (FIRST AND LAST) IMPRESSION

Learning Objective

To develop confidence in your relationships and daily interaction with others. In this chapter, you will learn to use the six S's and proper body language to make a lasting good impression on the people you meet and spend time with.

Introduction

Most of us want to make a good impression. Researchers tell us that it takes only a few seconds to make a first impression, but it takes several additional interactions to change someone's bad impression of us. In this lesson, you will discover a successful way to make a good first and lasting impression every time by learning how to present yourself properly to others.

IT TAKES AS LITTLE AS FIFTEEN SECONDS TO MAKE A FIRST IMPRESSION, BUT IT MAY TAKE THE REST OF YOUR LIFE TO CHANGE A BAD ONE.

THE SIX S'S

Every time you meet someone new and even when you greet an old friend, you are making some kind of an impression. To make a favorable impact on others, you need to know and practice the six S's: Stand. Smile. See their eyes. Shake hands. Say your name. Say their name back to them. Whether meeting or greeting, each of these actions make up your calling card, and everyone makes an impression—good or bad.

When the six S's become a habit, you will be free to focus on the things that are truly important because you will have more confidence in how you present yourself. You will no longer have to be self-conscious or worry about making a good impression. Armed with these skills, you will fulfill one of God's purposes for your life—reaching out to others.

When you learn and practice the six S's, you will unlock one of the secret codes of good manners and personal confidence. Why is it a secret code? Because few people will tell you when you fail to make a good impression. Some things are best learned at home or in class.

STAND

The first S is *stand.* If possible, always stand to meet or greet someone who is standing. There are exceptions, of course, such as when you are sitting at a crowded table in a restaurant. In this case, to stand might be disruptive and distracting to others.

SMILE

The second S is *smile.* Always smile. You may have heard that it takes only fourteen muscles to smile and more than seventy to frown. And a smile can be heard in any language. A deaf person can hear it, and a blind person can see it because there will be a lift in the person's voice. Try saying hello to your practice partner without smiling; then try smiling as you say hello to him or her. Do you see and hear the difference?

> If you see someone without a smile, give him one of yours.

SEE THEIR EYES

The third S is *see their eyes.* Looking others in the eye is difficult for some people. If you have trouble with this, or if you feel like you are staring at someone, try simply focusing on their face by looking from their eyes to their mouth and around their face. But don't look at the floor or at your surroundings. When you smile and look a person in the eye, you are giving them a gift—a gift of yourself and your complete attention.

PROPER HANDSHAKE

SHAKE HANDS

The fourth S is *shake hands.* Shaking hands in our country is a time-honored tradition dating back to the Old West when America was settled by men who carried guns. To show they were a friend and not an enemy, pioneers offered their empty hand. Thus, the handshake was invented, and that is why we do not kiss cheeks or rub noses when we meet others in our society, as people do in other countries.

A proper handshake is the same for males and females—firm but not painful; comfortable but not wimpy and fish-like. Practice this with a partner. Extend your right hand in a horizontal position with your thumb pointing upward and your fingers together. Allow the web between your thumb and index finger to meet the web of your partner's right hand while you grasp their hand and gently shake it.

Practice shaking hands with different partners (who know you are practicing). If you notice your partner giving you a wimpy or a crushing handshake, remind him or her as they learn the proper way. Practice sessions are a good way for each partner to critique the other. To criticize outside the session is very bad manners, unless your partner asks you to do so.

SAY YOUR NAME

The fifth S is *say your name.* With your partner, practice exchanging names. Say, "Hello! My name is _____. It's nice to meet you." If you have a difficult name to pronounce, speak it slowly and distinctly. Try pausing between your first and last names. If your name is something difficult, such as "Warbolosklowsi," you may have to repeat it. Be patient and gentle. You have known your name since birth, but this may be the first time the other person has heard it.

SAY THE OTHER PERSON'S NAME

The sixth and last S is *say their name back to them.* Say, "Hello, Mary (or Jim, or Mr. Smith or Mrs. Anthony)." It's usually not necessary to repeat both the other person's first and last names, unless you are unsure that you heard it correctly. If you are in doubt about whether it is proper to call someone by their first name, always use their last name because they can always say "Oh, just call me Joe" if they prefer that you call them by their first name.

Which one of the six S's is the most difficult for you to remember? Most people have trouble with the last one. For some reason, it's not easy to remember to repeat the other person's name. Sometimes it's difficult to remember a new person's name when a mutual friend introduces us. It may be that we are so focused on ourselves and what we will say next that we do not really hear the name, much less remember it. Repeating someone's name helps store it in our memory bank—and it makes the other person feel good.

> # WHEN YOU REPEAT SOMEONE'S NAME BACK TO THEM, IT'S LIKE GIVING THEM A GIFT.

PRACTICE, PRACTICE, PRACTICE

Practice with a partner. Stand, smile, see his or her eyes, shake hands, and say:

James: "Hello, my name is James Wesley."

Mary: "Hello, James. I'm Mary Anderson. It's nice to meet you, James. My family and I just moved here."

James: "I'm glad to meet you, too, Mary. I would be glad to introduce you to some of my friends."

Notice that each person repeats the other person's name.
Now practice with your teacher:

Teacher: "Hello, I'm Melinda Tanner, the librarian."

Student: "Hello, Mrs. Tanner. My name is James Wesley. I'm the new student body president."

Teacher: "I'm glad to meet you, James. I've heard good things about you."

Never say, "I've heard a lot about you" without adding something nice.

Notice that in these conversations, each person shared a little more information than simply their name. Doing so makes it easier to carry on a conversation after exchanging names. Notice also that James did not call the librarian by her first name; he correctly chose to use a title and the last name: Mrs. Tanner.

"O' would that we could see ourselves as others see us."
—Robert Burns

BODY LANGUAGE

Making a good impression also means that you look good—you are clean, neat, poised, and using the proper body language. What is body language? Everything you do with your hands, arms, legs, and face. The way you sit, the way you stand, your facial expression, hand gestures—it's all part of how you communicate with other people.

What does it mean when a parent puts both hands on his or her hips while staring intently at you? Anger, perhaps? What does it mean when you turn your head away from someone who is talking to you? Right. You are not paying attention. If you cross your arms across your chest with your hands tucked under your arms, you will look mad, cold, and unfriendly. However, if you cross your arms with your hands in plain sight, resting on top of your arms, you will have an open, friendly, approachable appearance.

At your teacher's instructions, demonstrate the above postures with a practice partner. (For more information on body language, poise, demeanor, and image, read the book *Social Skills Survival Guide* by June Hines Moore.)

REVIEW

1. Why are first impressions so important?

2. Name the six S's.

3. Name at least three reasons you should always repeat someone's name when you are introduced.

4. When is the only appropriate time to correct someone's manners?

5. Why is it a good idea to give the other person a little more information about yourself than simply your name?

LESSON TWO

MAKING INTRODUCTIONS/ CONVERSATION

COMMUNICATING WITH EASE

Learning Objective

To become skillful in making conversation with your friends and new acquaintances. (According to www.Dictionary.com, the definition of *conversation* is the spoken exchange of thoughts, opinions, and feelings.) You will also learn how to properly introduce one person to another.

Introduction

Some people have the gift of gab, while others do not. Some people can carry on a conversation with a signpost, but the truth is that most of us have a little trouble talking to people we don't know well—and sometimes even to people we have known for a long time. Are you good at small talk? If not, you will enjoy learning and practicing the helpful tips in this lesson.

> ## "The greater the man, the greater the courtesy."
> ### —Alfred Lord Tennyson

MAKING PROPER INTRODUCTIONS

The first rule of making conversation is to make introductions where necessary. Always try to introduce a friend to others, even when you forget the rules or cannot remember everyone's names.

The most important rule about making introductions is making the effort. Have you ever been with a friend who seemed to know everyone but never bothered to introduce you to the others? How did that make you feel? Uncomfortable? Out of place? Many people do not know how to make introductions or perhaps they are afraid to try, so they simply do not make the effort, which is the worst choice of all.

Now that you know the six S's and are comfortable introducing yourself to others, you are ready to learn and practice the rules for introducing one friend to another friend and making conversation. Do not worry about remembering names. We will learn some remedies for that problem.

MAKING AN INTRODUCTION

A good rule of thumb is to introduce the lesser person to the greater. But try to remember: You are not judging the person's character; you are simply showing respect. Here are some easy-to-remember guidelines:

- Introduce the younger person to the older person.

- Introduce a gentleman to a lady.

- Introduce a less-distinguished person to a more-distinguished person.

- Give first and last names, or at least give each person a name they can use to address the person they are meeting. Instead of saying "Grandma," say "My grandmother, Mrs. Dailey."

The trick is to decide first who is older, who is female, or who is in a more important position. Once you decide which of the individuals is in the honored position, look at that person, call him or her by name, and give the name of the other person. (The less-important individual will be younger, or male, or simply the person in a less-important position. For instance, a teacher should be honored over a student, even if the teacher is male, and the student is a teen-aged female.) Then address the lesser-important person and give him/her the full name (or title) of the more-important person of the two.

Here is an example of how to introduce a friend to your mom:

Say, "Mom, this is my friend Tom Adams from school. He's on my soccer team."

Then say to your friend, "Tom, this is my mom, Mrs. Neal."

Your mom will say something like: "Hello, Tom, it's nice to meet you." Then Tom will say, "Hi, Mrs. Neal. I'm glad to meet you too."

If your name is Phil and you are introduced to someone as "Bill," simply say, "It's Phil" as you are shaking hands. Repeating your name to get it right is one of the few times you can politely correct someone else's mistake.

PRACTICE

Now that you know the rules, you are ready to practice with two partners. Here are some situations to help you practice.

1. **Introduce your young male coach and your male pastor.**

2. **Introduce your grandmother and one of your mom's friends. Both are adult females.**

3. **Introduce your brother, Michael (same last name as yours), and your friend Tom Adams, who is on your soccer team.**

4. **Introduce your friend from church, Kristen Carpenter, and your friend, Tom Adams. Both are about the same age.**

Here are a few additional tips to make your introductions go more smoothly:

- Always address an adult with a title (such as Mr., Mrs., Dr., or Coach) before their last name.

- Try to include some additional information about each person so they will be able to have a conversation.

- Give both first and last names when you can.

- If you have a job, remember that an adult customer is always the honored person, even over your boss.

- If you find yourself with one friend (for instance at a party), and a whole group of your friends known only to you approaches, it is not necessary to repeat everyone's name in the group. Simply say the name of the friend already with you. The members of the group can introduce themselves individually later.

REMEMBERING NAMES

Almost everyone has trouble remembering names, but that should not keep you from making your friends and family feel more comfortable by introducing them. When you see an acquaintance approaching whose name you cannot remember, extend your hand and say, "Hi, I'm Mary Wilkes from church camp last year." Hopefully, the other person will repeat his or her name for you. If you are not so fortunate, simply say, "Sorry, but my mind has just gone blank; you will have to help me out" or "I know we've met. Please tell me your name again." The secret is to make the situation your predicament and not make it your acquaintance's problem.

If you do not understand the other person's name when you are introduced, simply say, "I didn't quite get your name" or "Could you repeat your name for me, please?"

THE CARDINAL RULE OF CONVERSATION:

Never say anything hurtful or mean-spirited to the person with whom you are talking. And never say anything mean-spirited about someone else.

TIPS FOR TALKING

Communication is a lot more than tossing some words out in public. It is a skill you can learn. Think of it as playing a game with a ball. One person talks awhile and then listens (tosses the ball) for the other person to talk. However, when one person talks more than thirty to forty seconds before tossing the ball, he or she is making a speech. You may be surprised to see how long a time that really is.

As you practice making conversation with a partner or with a group of friends, here are some important tips to remember:

• Listen closely while the other person is talking. Interruptions are annoying. To show you are paying attention, look at the person's face and not at your surroundings.

Former secretary of state Dean Rusk once said, "The best way to persuade others is with our ears." In other words, if you want people to listen to you, first be a good listener. Remember, nobody cares how much you know until they know how much you care.

- Good general topics for conversation with someone your own age include: family, school, hobbies, after-school jobs, movies, books, entertainment, vacations, church activities, places you have lived or visited, pets, sports, plans for the future, and how you know mutual friends.

- Do not ask personal questions that you would not want someone to ask you. For instance, *How much do you weigh?* or *How much money does your father make?*

- When you are around food, avoid subjects such as dieting, gory information, or argumentative topics such as politics—anything that may lead to unpleasantness.

- Be sincere, but make at least one nice or complimentary remark to your partner in conversation. For example, you can congratulate someone on an achievement, comment on a recent success, or mention how nice they look.

- Do not embarrass someone with flattery, which is usually exaggerated praise.

- Accept compliments graciously without making excuses. Say, "Thank you" or "You are kind to notice."

- If you disagree with your partner in conversation, be pleasant and respectful. Keep your voice low as you give your opinion. Instead of saying "You are wrong," you can say, "We seem to disagree about that" or "It looks like we have different opinions on that subject" and move on to something else.

- Develop a sense of humor about yourself. Never laugh when someone else is being made fun of or ridiculed. But learn to laugh at yourself. For instance: "I did the dumbest thing the other day . . ."

- Do not be a complainer or a criticizer.

- Do not be a know-it-all. Simply because you know something does not mean that you have to tell it.

- If you are asked a question you consider too personal, do not react in horror. Turn it into something funny. For instance, if someone asks how many dates you've been on, simply say, "Not as many as I would have liked!"

• Ask open-ended questions. These are questions that require more than a simple yes-or-no answer or a single-word answer. Examples: "What do you hear from our old friend Bill?" or "What are your favorite books?" A closed-ended question might be "How many brothers do you have?" That question can be answered with one number and probably no other comments.

• Do not interrupt someone's story to correct their facts. It probably does not matter if the date was last June or last July.

• Be honest without being unkind. If your sister asks how you like her hair, and you think it looks hideous, you can say, "Oh, I see you got a new style" or "I see you got it cut."

• Do not try to inflate your own image by running down someone else.

PRACTICE

Now practice making conversation with a partner. Here are some good conversation starters: the latest high-tech gadget, a new DVD or CD, the recent sporting event at your school, the new fashions for the spring season, the latest episode of your favorite TV show, or the upcoming youth activity at your church. Let's get started.

1. Choose a topic from suggestions in this chapter, or if you know your partner well, you may select another subject of interest to both of you. You and your partner will have a total of three to five minutes to talk about your chosen subject. One of you will begin talking while holding a ball. After a few sentences, the speaker will gently toss the ball to his or her conversation partner. Your instructor will monitor how long each person talks before tossing the ball to his or her partner. It is a good idea to pose a question as you toss the ball to your partner when it is his or her turn to talk, but it is not obligatory.

2. Change partners, choose another topic, and create a new conversation.

REVIEW

1. When is it acceptable to ignore introducing people? Why?

2. How do you decide who is the more important person when making an introduction?

3. Give an example of something you can say to a person when you cannot remember his or her name.

4. Why is it rude to interrupt, even if you know the correct answer or the right way to do something?

5. Name some topics that are not pleasant to talk about around the dining table.

6. How do you know if you are making "flattering" comments?

7. Never laugh at others, only _____.

8. (True or False) Accept compliments by saying "Thank you."

9. Give an example of an open-ended question.

10. (True or False) Telling the truth does not mean you have to be brutally honest and hurt someone's feelings. You can always find something nice to say.

LESSON THREE

THE DATING GAME

A GUIDE TO GUY/GIRL SOCIAL INTERACTION

Learning Objective

To gain useful knowledge as you grow socially in purity and maturity.

Introduction

The *World Book Encyclopedia Dictionary* says a date is "a person of the opposite sex with whom a social appointment is made." For example, your parents may enjoy a "date night" together each week. You might want to ask them why this is important to them, even though they live in the same house and see one another every day.

Your parents have probably established rules in your home for when you will go out with friends of the opposite sex, probably in groups at first. If not, you need to have a discussion with your parents to clarify their expectations.

In this lesson, you will learn some important and helpful tips on what is expected of you socially as a young woman or a young man. When you know the basic rules, you can more easily enjoy relating to people outside your family circle.

The first get-togethers for any boy/girl relationship should begin in a group that your parents have arranged or approved. It is important that you have caring, interested adults there to help you as you enter this new stage in your life.

No matter your age, there are a few dos and don'ts for both girls and guys whether you are in a group setting or in a one-on-one social occasion when you are older. If you have any questions or disagreement about any of these guidelines, do not hesitate to ask your instructor. Now is the time to learn the skills you will use the rest of your life.

After this lesson, you will have an opportunity to interview an adult or married couple whose relationship you admire and trust. Before you venture out on your assignment, your instructor will give you a list of questions to ask in the interview. After the interview, you will come back and share what you have learned.

DOS AND DON'TS FOR GUYS AND GIRLS:

- Never break a date or social commitment so that you can go with someone else who asks later.

- Be a good sport and have a sense of humor, but laugh only at "clean" comments or stories.

- Show a sincere interest in the accomplishments of the person(s) you are with.

- Be willing to try something new if the group plans a fun, wholesome activity that you have never done before. If you find you are not good at it, simply laugh at yourself. Hardly anyone is good at everything.

- Say "thank you" when someone pays you a compliment. Do not giggle or duck your head and stare at your shoes.

- Be a good listener. Pay attention. Ask appropriate questions or say, "Tell me more about that."

- As a guy, do not neglect or ignore your partner, especially if you are paired off as part of a larger group. You should not leave your partner sitting or standing alone with no one to talk to, unless you briefly excuse yourself to get refreshments for the two of you or if you must go to the restroom.

- Do not be possessive.

- Do not be loud or call undue attention to yourself.

- Do not criticize, gossip, or betray a confidence. You can find better things to talk about. (One definition of gossip and criticism is anything that makes another person look bad.)

A YOUNG LADY'S IDEAL DATE

When your parents agree you are old enough to date, the following may be helpful. One young lady named Karen provided this account of what she considers an ideal date:

My ideal date calls me about a week in advance. He tells me where we are going and with whom. When he arrives, I greet him at the door because if he honked the horn, I would not respond. I invite him into the house to meet my parents, and we chat for a little while.

During our time together, he opens doors for me, pulls out my chair as we sit down and when we rise. He treats me like a lady and always introduces me to any of his friends whom I may not know. He opens the car door for me, both getting in and out of the car.

He is neat and courteous, and has a good sense of humor without being silly or crude. He talks mostly to me and does not leave me alone to talk to other guys or girls. When the evening is over, he walks me to the door where we say good night. He tells me he had a nice time, and I tell him the same, or at least I thank him for asking me.

> "Nothing is so strong as gentleness, nothing so gentle as strength."
> —St. Francis of Assisi

A YOUNG MAN'S IDEAL DATE

A young man named Richard gave this account of what he considers the ideal date:

> *My ideal date gives me her answer to my invitation as soon as she can. She does not leave me hanging until it is too late to ask someone else.*
>
> *She is ready to go (or almost) and greets me at the door with a big smile. She invites me in to meet or visit with her parents. She then tells me what time her parents want her to be home. She behaves like a lady at all times without giggling or acting silly. She stands to the side and out of the way from doors so that I can open them for her, including car doors, and she quietly says thank you.*
>
> *She is a good sport about participating in group activities. She does not become sullen or pout to show her disappointment or discontent. She is agreeable even when she is not very good at a game or activity. She doesn't gossip or talk about old boyfriends, and she doesn't pay a lot of attention to other guys at the party.*
>
> *When the evening is over, I walk her to her front door, and she smiles and thanks me for inviting her.*

> **"Rudeness is the weak man's imitation of strength."**
> —Eric Hoffer

WHEN THE YOUNG LADY DOES THE INVITING

On certain occasions it is appropriate for a young lady to extend an invitation to a young man. For example, your school or youth group at church may have a "Sadie Hawkins" day, which is an old tradition that usually takes place in early springtime. Or perhaps the young woman needs an escort to a prom or banquet, usually from outside her school or church. In other words, it is generally not a good idea for a girl to invite a guy who could invite her to the same event.

On such an occasion, the girl is expected to provide the money or buy the tickets, but it is common practice to hand the money or tickets to her escort before they leave her house or soon thereafter. Sometimes, a guy who is invited will insist on paying for everything. The two of you should come to an agreement before that night, or before you leave her house, and not squabble in front of others about who pays.

The guy and girl should behave as though he had invited her. In other words, he still comes to her home to get her and performs all the manners of a gentleman, such as opening doors, etc.

WHEN THE ANSWER IS NO

Whether you are the guy or the girl, being rejected or turned down for an invitation can be painful. But remember, it happens to everyone. Let's say a guy wants to escort a certain young lady to an event, but when he calls, he learns she has already been asked. She should say, "Thank you so much for asking me, but someone invited me a few days ago. Maybe I'll see you there." He should take it like a man and not ask questions about who or why. He should say, "I'll try to call you sooner next time," and end the call in a positive, upbeat manner.

"MANNERS ARE A SENSITIVE AWARENESS OF THE FEELINGS OF OTHERS. IF YOU HAVE THAT AWARENESS, YOU HAVE GOOD MANNERS."

—EMILY POST

WHEN YOUR DATE IS NOT QUITE READY

Men, if your date is not quite ready when you arrive, her parents may entertain you in the living room. If they are busy with something else, here are a few things you should keep in mind:

- Do not snoop or take liberties with your surroundings.

- Do not take it literally when told to "make yourself at home."

- Respect the furniture. Use a coaster if someone gives you something to drink while you wait. Never put your feet on tables or chairs.

- Do not turn up the volume of the TV, radio, or CD player.

- Do not go into any other room. If you must go to the restroom, wait until you can ask someone if you may and where it is.

- Do not snoop around in drawers or pick things up to look at them.

- Stand when the girl or the mom enters the room.

- If the dad stays to talk to you, let him do most of the talking, but be ready to answer any questions he might ask. Say, "Yes, sir" and "No, sir."

PUBLIC MANNERS

PUTTING THE GOLDEN RULE INTO ACTION

Learning Objective

To acquire specific people skills to help you avoid public embarrassment.

Introduction

In a public place, your manners are always on display and public embarrassment can be especially painful. But when you know the rules and practice the Golden Rule—do to others what you would have them do to you—you can avoid making a *faux pas*. This chapter is designed to help you become more aware of your surroundings on a daily basis and to always take into account the feelings of those around you.

An important watchword for this lesson—and life—is "defer." It means to yield, to give way for others, to think of others before yourself. For instance, in our society, guys are expected to defer to girls, as in letting them go through a door first. Guys and girls alike should defer to older people, as in offering their seat to an elderly person on a crowded bus.

It's hard to go wrong when you make an effort to put others' needs and interests before your own.

> "YOUR MANNERS ARE ALWAYS UNDER EXAMINATION BY COMMITTEES LITTLE SUSPECTED ... AWARDING OR DENYING YOU VERY HIGH PRIZES WHEN YOU LEAST THINK OF IT."—Ralph Waldo Emerson

REASONS FOR THE RULES

Sometimes it may seem that the rules of good manners are just a bunch of regulations that someone made up to make us all miserable trying to be prim and proper. However, there is a reason behind every rule of etiquette, and this lesson provides an interesting glimpse into some of those reasons. Most have a practical purpose, as you will see.

The following rules of conduct involve men holding doors for women, the proper way to enter an elevator, and even the proper way to pull out a chair for a lady. See if you can determine the reason for some of these rules. Your instructor has the answers and the reasons. If you are working through this manual on your own, the answers appear in the teacher's pages on pages 83–84.

1. When walking with a girl, a guy should walk on the street side of the sidewalk.

2. To escort a girl for any reason, a guy extends his arm bent at the elbow for her to hold. She loops her hand inside the space he has created. He does not take hold of her arm.

3. When going through a door that pulls toward him, the guy opens the door and holds it for the girl to go through first. Then he follows her as he holds the door for others who may be following (unless there is a crowd of people, in which case he should hand the door off to the next guy in line).

4. When going through a push door, the guy pushes the door open and goes through the doorway first. Then he holds the door for the girl to pass through.

5. A guy should allow the girl to enter and exit an uncrowded elevator first, while he blocks the door with his hand to prevent it from closing on her. When the elevator is crowded, people nearest the door get off first.

6. If you are standing near the control panel, you should be ready to hold the "open door" button for others entering or leaving, and you should offer to punch in the floor numbers for others on the elevator.

7. The guy holds the chair for the girl on his right, who slides in from the left of her chair seat. He also helps the lady on his left if there is no gentleman to assist her. A gentleman does not sit down until all the ladies are seated at the table. After the girl sits, she grips the sides of the seat of her chair and helps her escort lift the chair as he takes a firm grip of each side of the back of the chair, and pushes it back under the table.

8. When ascending escalators or stairs, the girl goes up first. The guy follows her. When coming down escalators or stairs, the guy goes first. The girl follows him.

9. Guys always remove their hats and caps when there is a roof over their head. In other words, no guy should wear a cap or hat as he enters a restaurant or other building. (Jewish temples are one exception.)

10. In a movie theater or church when there is no usher present, the guy leads the way down the aisle. He stands outside the chosen row while the girl goes in first to choose a seat. He follows.

11. When exiting a row of filled seats, one should avoid stepping on toes or bending forward allowing his or her derriere to be in the face of those they are passing. (I told you learning manners should be fun!)

> **MANNERS TRIVIA:**
>
> **IN MASSACHUSETTS IT IS AGAINST THE LAW TO EAT PEANUTS IN CHURCH.**

ENTERTAINMENT COURTESIES

Now let's look at some hints on how to be courteous in entertainment venues. Sporting events have their own culture and rules for acceptable behavior, but the Golden Rule still applies. Whether you are attending the movies, a play, or some other performance, the same basic rules apply. Here are some things you need to know to avoid embarrassing yourself or offending someone else. These manners are best learned at home; instructions will not be available once you arrive.

- Arrive on time.

- Before the show, do not whistle, laugh boisterously, shout, or yell out someone's name. Keep your voice low, and do not draw attention to yourself.

- If you have a pager or a cell phone, set it to "vibrate" or turn it off.

- Always rise for the national anthem and for the anthem of another country.

- Keep your feet on the floor, not on the seats around you.

- If your cough becomes a prolonged episode, remove yourself from the auditorium. After you stop coughing, return to your seat during an intermission or other appropriate time.

- Do not talk, boo, hiss, groan, gasp, or make other noises that might disturb others.

- Do not hum, sing along, or keep time with your fingers or feet unless you are invited to do so by the performers.

- Do not spit chewing gum on the floor or stick it under seats. Wrap it in paper and dispose of it in a waste receptacle.

- Clean up after yourself, properly discarding tissues, candy wrappers, popcorn boxes, and soda containers.

- When attending a formal musical performance, there are very specific times when you should applaud, and doing so at the wrong time can be very embarrassing. Follow the cues of more experienced concertgoers around you.

MANNERS ON THE ROAD

If you are a passenger in a car, you should ask permission from your fellow passengers before opening or closing windows or adjusting the heat, the air conditioning, the radio, or the CD player. If you must use your cell phone, ask for permission.

If you are driving a car, always take care to park appropriately. Avoid taking up two parking spaces. When you parallel park, make sure the cars in front and behind you can easily pull out of their spaces.

If another driver is rude, do not respond by showing anger or making any gestures. If you do, the other driver's manners will not likely improve and you may be putting yourself in danger if he or she chooses to retaliate.

GOOD MANNERS WITH THE DISABLED

When speaking of a person with a disability, it is impolite to call them "handicapped." Most individuals with a disability prefer that we think of who they are and not for what they are unable to do. Here are some things to keep in mind:

- Never point or stare at anyone who looks different in any way.

- Avoid using terms that suggest your feelings about the disabled, such as pity, disease, or their obvious dependency.

- If you think assistance may be needed, always ask if you can help, and wait for an answer. People with disabilities pride themselves on being as independent as possible, but sometimes they will welcome your assistance.

- Do not appear to be impatient or offended if your offer to help is not accepted.

- If your offer to help is accepted, ask politely what you can do.

CHURCH MANNERS

Always enter a church quietly and reverently in time for the beginning of the service. Guys should remove their hats or caps before entering. If you are late, wait in the foyer for a break in the service when an usher may seat you.

In churches not your own, be respectful and observant, careful to follow the ritual as much as you can. You may join in the worship, but you should take communion only if a clergyman invites you do so. If you feel uncomfortable participating in the functions of worship, you may refrain, but always respect others' beliefs, sacraments, ordinances, and customs. Think of yourself as a visitor in someone's home.

PDAS, LAPTOP COMPUTERS, AND PERSONAL GAME DEVICES

A laptop computer can be a useful tool unless it annoys the people near you who must listen to the constant clicking of the keyboard. It is polite to ask those nearby if the noise disturbs them. If they say yes, excuse yourself, if possible, and move to a private or semi-private place.

The same advice applies to using your PDA or game-playing device. Remember that it is considered rude to ignore those around you while you devote your full attention to an inanimate object.

DEALING WITH RUDE PEOPLE

We all encounter rude people from time to time. We must remember that some offenders do not mean to be rude; they perhaps have never had the opportunity to learn good manners. Therefore, we must refrain from retaliation and remember to set a good example.

> "An honest 'Excuse me' is the grease that eases the friction of human interaction. It's the bumper between bodies on the verge of collision. It's a little peace offering in the daily combat of urban life."
>
> —Mary Schmich

THE JOB INTERVIEW

PUTTING YOUR BEST FOOT FORWARD

Learning Objectives

To effectively present yourself as a prospective employee and increase your chances of getting the job you want.

Introduction

As reported in *Today's Office* magazine, when a young intern in a multimillion-dollar corporation was not promoted, he asked his boss why and was told that the problem was his manners, his business etiquette. With the training and interview experience in this lesson, you will be prepared to confidently apply for the job you want.

Following your instructor's directions, you will use this ad to practice applying for a job:

> **WANTED: Sales Associate.** People skills and good work ethic needed. Sales background helpful but not required. Call for interview appointment or send résumé. Calvary Christian Bookstore, 555-1234.

"ABOUT 15 PERCENT OF ONE'S FINANCIAL AND CAREER SUCCESS IS DUE TO TECHNICAL SKILLS, WHILE THE REMAINING 85 PERCENT IS DUE TO PEOPLE SKILLS."

—Sherwin-Williams Company News

FIVE WAYS TO GET AN APPOINTMENT FOR AN INTERVIEW

With your teacher's help, fill in the blank. If you are working through this manual alone, the answers appear on page 85.

1. _____ to introduce and recommend you.

2. Call for an _____ for an interview.

3. Contact the personnel office and pick up _____.

4. Send a _____ with a _____.

5. Apply online. Make certain that all necessary _____ is clearly included at the top of the page. Your application may be scanned and valuable information may not print near the top or bottom of the paper.

ANSWERING AN AD BY PHONE

Introduce yourself as follows:

> "My name is Lisa Mathers. I am calling to request an appointment for an interview regarding your advertisement for a sales associate."
>
> "I will transfer you to Ms. Hargreaves."
>
> "Thank you."
>
> Repeat your original information to the person to whom you are transferred.

FILLING OUT A JOB APPLICATION

Be prepared to give the following information:

- Today's date

- Position you are applying for

- Date you are available to begin work

- Your full name

- Your address, including the zip code

- Your telephone number (day, night, and cellular)

- Your e-mail address

- Your age

- Your education, including the name of the school(s), the years you've attended, and your grade-point average

- Your employment history, including any jobs you've held, the name(s) of your supervisor(s), your job title, the dates of your employment, and the hourly rate you were paid

- Any special skills you can bring to the job

- Three personal references (including two non-relatives), their addresses, and their phone numbers. (A personal reference is someone who can knowledgeably vouch for your character. Be sure to obtain permission from any person before giving out his or her name and contact information.)

Letter to Request a Referral

Use this sample or create your own to request a referral or recommendation from a non-relative. You may also call the individual to request a referral.

Dear Mr. (Mrs.) Banner,

You knew me as your (paper boy/babysitter) for three years. My parents are Stephen and Melissa Gray.

I am applying for a job at Calvary Christian Bookstore. If the employer contacts you, I would really appreciate it if you could recommend me for the job.

In a few days I will call to get your decision or you may call me at 555-0000.

Thank you very much.

Yours truly,

(Your first and last name)

Do I Need a Résumé?

If this is your first job experience, then probably not. Most entry-level jobs open to teens do not require a résumé. The purpose of a résumé is to favorably describe your education, accomplishments, skills, and experience to a prospective employer. If the job you are applying for requires a résumé, visit your local library, where you will find many excellent resources on how to write a résumé and cover letter.

THE INTERVIEW

Here are a few things to keep in mind during the interview:

1. First, introduce yourself to the receptionist: "My name is _____ and I have an appointment at 4:00 with Mr. Markham." (Be prepared to spell your name for the person at the reception desk.)

---

2. Say "thank you" when the receptionist asks you to be seated. Then sit down and wait quietly. If a trade or news magazine is on a table, you may pick it up to read. Don't try to carry on a conversation with the receptionist, who is probably busy, unless he or she initiates it.

3. If you are offered refreshment, say "No, thank you" or "I wouldn't care for anything, but thank you." (You might spill something.)

4. If anyone approaches you in the waiting area, you should stand to your feet.

5. Say "thank you" when you are ushered into the interviewer's office.

6. When the receptionist introduces you or announces your name, immediately extend your hand and say, "How do you do, Mr. Blackstone?" or "Hello, Mr. Blackstone. I am Jermaine Smith."

7. Wait for the interviewer to offer his hand first, but have your right hand free and ready to grasp his in a firm handshake. (If you are not announced when you are ushered in and the interviewer does not introduce himself, extend your hand and say, "Hello, Mr. Markham. I am Stephanie Suarez.")

8. Wait for the interviewer to ask you to be seated. Sit erect near the front of the chair. Don't slump back in a relaxed fashion. If you are not told where to hang your top coat, place it over the back of your chair or on a nearby chair. Never place anything on the interviewer's desk. (Never remove your suit jacket or sport coat.)

9. If you are offered some refreshment, politely say, "No, thank you." (Once you are in the office, you may be offered something again, as you were in the reception area.)

10. Let the interviewer begin the conversation. Remember, you are there to sell yourself as meeting the job requirements of the employer, not to fulfill your hopes and dreams. If the interviewer says, "Tell me about yourself," that is your cue to talk about your job experience and/or qualifications. You should know them well and be able to explain why you are the right person for the job.

11. If Mr. Markham asks why you want to work for him or the company, tell him how much you like talking about books and meeting people who like to read books (or reasons for responding to the ad other than you saw it in the paper).

12. If the interviewer asks what you would like to know about working there, inquire, for example, about using your computing skills or organizational skills such as taking inventory and shelving books. You may ask about advancement opportunities, but clearly show that you realize you must prove your abilities and skills before you could expect a promotion.

13. Ask intelligent questions about your role on the work team, such as to whom you would report or who your supervisor would be. Ask what your primary responsibilities would be. Smile, don't frown when these duties are stated.

14. Don't ask about breaks, lunchtime, and days off. You can ask those questions after you get the job. Don't complain or gossip about past employers or work conditions. Let the interviewer bring up the subject of salary.

Some questions you may be asked during the interview include:

Interviewer: "In addition to your sales-floor duties, you would have to keep detailed records and do some legwork. How do you feel about doing such routine work?"

Answer: "I am willing to do whatever is required. There has been routine work in all my jobs, including running a paper route (or babysitting). I know that a certain amount of routine is a part of every job."

Interviewer: "We use_____ at this store. Are you familiar with that procedure?"

Answer: "I am somewhat familiar with that procedure, and I'd like to learn more. I feel sure I can adapt what I know about ___ _____ procedure from my last job." (Or, "I haven't been trained in that procedure, but I am more than willing to learn.")

Interviewer: "All employment at this store is on a probationary basis for three months. Are you willing to work here on a trial basis?"

Answer: "Yes, sir (or ma'am). I would like to have that opportunity and feel that I can prove my worth to you in that time."

Interviewer: "Why did you apply for a job at this store?"

Answer: "My future plans include a career in sales or management. With my past jobs and the schoolwork I've completed, I have learned to appreciate the opportunities a job in your store could offer."

> "There is no accomplishment so easy to acquire as politeness, and none more profitable."
>
> —George Bernard Shaw

Preparing for the Interview

Your preparation for the interview is as important as the interview itself. Write and carry with you the date, time, location, and the name of the interviewer. Allow yourself plenty of time to get there. Be dressed appropriately and know everything you can about the company or business where you are applying.

THE INTERVIEW STEP-BY-STEP

Arriving only a few minutes early, approach the receptionist with only a folder or briefcase holding your résumé, if you have one. Women may carry a shoulder-strap purse on their left shoulder; they should never carry a clutch bag because the right hand must always be free and ready to shake hands.

Remember to use the six S's.

Applicant: Hello, my name is _____ and I have an appointment with _____. (If the receptionist has his or her hands free, you may extend your hand for a firm handshake.) I am a few minutes early, so I will just wait.

Receptionist: Hello, yes, we were expecting you. Please have a seat over there.

Applicant: Thank you. (Take your seat, placing your overcoat over the back of your chair.)

Receptionist: Mr./Ms. _____ will see you now. Please come with me.

Applicant: Thank you. (You follow behind him/her. This is one time the man does not open doors for the lady unless she steps aside and waits, expecting you to do so. The receptionist opens the door and you practice the six S's, waiting for the interviewer to extend a hand first, but obviously expecting him or her to do so.)

Receptionist: (introducing you) Mr./Ms. _____, this is _____. He is here to interview for our job opening.

Applicant: Hello, Mr./Ms._____. (Remain standing until told where to sit. Once seated, ladies place their hands in their lap, and guys place their hands on their legs. Putting them on the arms of the chair may make you look too relaxed.)

Interviewer: Hello, _____. How are you? Please have a seat there.

Applicant: I'm fine. Thank you.

Interviewer: Tell me something about yourself.

Applicant: (Recount some of your work history and/or education and interests that you have memorized in preparation for such a question.)

Interviewer: Why do you think you want to work here at Calvary Christian Bookstore?

Applicant: Well, sir, I like to read and I like people, so I think I would enjoy telling customers about the good books here.

Interviewer: What skills or abilities do you have that would be useful to us here in the bookstore?

Applicant: (These may be computer skills, stocking experience, leadership offices in school, etc.)

Interviewer: Is this your first job?

Applicant: No, sir. Last summer I mowed lawns, which meant I handled money and showed my responsibility and dependability.

Interviewer: All employment at this store is on a probationary basis for three months. Are you willing to work here on a trial basis?

Applicant: Yes, sir: I would appreciate the opportunity to prove myself.

Interviewer: Do you have any questions?

Applicant: Would it be possible to get promoted after I work hard in whatever position I start in?

Interviewer: Yes, we have several levels of employment here. We can discuss the details later. Well, thank you for coming in. We'll let you know when the decision is made to fill the position.

Applicant: (You rise, shake his or her hand, and gather up your things.) Thank you for your time. I would really like to work here, and I think I could do a good job for you.

(Exit quietly, closing doors behind you and saying thank you to those in the outer office, especially the receptionist. Close the door gently but completely.) Unless you are told otherwise, you may call in a few days or a week to check the status of the position for which you applied.

THE FOLLOW-UP LETTER

Be sure to send the interviewer a thank-note or letter that same day, if possible. Write a follow-up letter similar to the one below:

Your address
The date

Mrs. Sara Nelson
Department Manager
Allied Associates
4209 Lancaster Street
Sante Fe, New Mexico 80059

Dear Mrs. Nelson:

Thank you for taking the time to interview me today about working for your company in the position of _____.
I feel that I could do a good job for you, and I would like to be a part of your organization.

I look forward to hearing from you.

Yours truly,

(Your first and last name)

LESSON SIX

WHAT TO WEAR

TIPS FOR LOOKING YOUR BEST

Learning Objective

To develop the knowledge and expertise you need to give you confidence in the way you dress.

Introduction

Whether you are going on a date, to church, to a school function, or to a college entrance or job interview, the way you dress says a lot about you. A haphazard appearance gives the impression that you are untidy and even careless. The way you dress shows how much you respect yourself and others.

In this lesson, you will choose from your closet what you would wear to an interview with a college dean of admissions or for a job interview as an entry-level office worker. You will make a list of items you may need to replace, such as a new shirt or tie, what you need to polish or have cleaned and pressed.

You might go with a parent to a very nice clothing store to learn about dressing appropriately. You may also want to visit a formal shop to learn about formal wear in preparation for a prom or a banquet where "Black Tie" is indicated on the invitation.

As mentioned earlier, you make a first impression on others within a few seconds after you come into view, so the way you package yourself is important. You want people to remember you for your wonderful personality or your social skills and not for your unkempt or disheveled appearance. It is not about buying expensive clothes, but about purchasing well-chosen, quality clothing and accessories.

Studies show that job applicants who dress appropriately are paid higher starting salaries, and that improper attire is often the reason applicants are turned down for a job. When applying for a job, dress as closely as you can to the way the best-dressed person there dresses. Some experts say to dress for the job or position you would like to have.

You may incorrectly assume that if no one says anything negative about your appearance, you are appropriately dressed. The truth is that if anyone says anything to you about your appearance, the damage to your overall image may have already been done.

> "Improper dress is the most common reason job candidates are eliminated."
> —John Molloy, *Dress for Success*

WHAT NOT TO WEAR

Here are some general dos and don'ts for job interviews, church attendance, and college entrance interviews. This list is not intended to be unjustly critical or a reflection on anyone's character. The items are simply inappropriate for college applicants, for the church sanctuary, and for job interviews. (One caveat: This list should not be used to exclude anyone from a church. It is for your personal use only.)

- the geeky or grunge look

- see-through blouses or dresses

- shirts or tops with an inappropriate message on them

- cutoff jeans or pants

- shorts

- strapless dresses

- bare midriffs

- jogging or "wind" suits

- platform-type shoes that make a slapping noise on a wooden floor

- clothing that is too tight

- clothes that drift downward from the waist

- sunglasses

- too many earrings or other jewelry (for girls); any jewelry for guys

- plunging necklines

- high heels that wobble and make the wearer tend to stumble

- mini-skirts

- a slip showing through the slits in a skirt

- lingerie-type clothing of any kind

- tight or unlined slacks that reveal the wearer's underpants

- chewing gum, toothpicks, candy, or drink

GROOMING

Tattoos cannot be removed easily, and they are highly discouraged. Good grooming and attention to detail are important. Even high-quality clothing is easily cheapened by neglect of daily grooming habits (showering, shaving, hairstyling, etc.) and proper hygiene, such as clean fingernails, nose, and ears.

"The critical factor in credibility is presenting the expected image. . . . Don't wear anything that will surprise the people you meet for a job interview."

—John Molloy, *Dress for Success*

USEFUL TIPS FOR THE GUYS

- Your shoes should be well polished.

- Guys wearing a suit must wear nice loafers or leather, lace-up shoes—no canvas or athletic footwear.

- For interviews, a spotless white shirt is your best bet.

- The tip of your tie should reach the middle of the belt buckle, not above the buckle, nor below it.

- Ties should not be so loud (regardless of how beautiful) that you are remembered for the parrot or ducks on your tie rather than for your knowledge or expertise.

- Good suit colors for guys are navy, charcoal, dark brown, and gray.

- Your socks should be long enough to cover the calf of your leg when you sit and cross your legs, with no exposed skin between the sock and the cuff or hem of the trouser leg.

- Shirt collars should button comfortably when two fingers are inserted between the collar and the neck of the wearer.

- Suits for guys are a little more formal and business-like than slacks and a sport coat, which are fine if that is the only type outfit available to you.

- Conforming and dressing to suit the occasion may not always be the most comfortable choice, but doing so is definitely the wisest choice. You do not want your appearance to be a shock or a distraction.

TIPS FOR YOUNG WOMEN

For a job or college interview, a young lady should wear a dress, a jacket dress, or a conservative suit—no jeans or slacks. Her shoes should be flats or low heels with no patterned hosiery or stockings with runs or snags. A small handbag or small shoulder purse is appropriate. A big bag is not.

Here are common mistakes girls sometimes make:

- Wearing too many accessories (distracting from their true self)

- Wearing a skirt shorter than one inch above the knee

- Earrings that are too long or too large

- Chipped nail polish, or long "witch" or decorated fingernails

- Grooming in public

- Too much makeup

- Too much perfume

- Hair constantly falling in their face

- Continually flipping or pulling at their hair

- Wearing their hair down in their eyes, making it difficult to see them

- Wearing clothing inappropriate for the occasion

HOW TO SHOP

When shopping for appropriate clothes, always go first to an expensive store known for its quality and fit to learn what the best clothing looks like. Then when you shop in a store that better fits your budget, you will know what to buy. Better quality clothing usually costs a little more but looks better for a longer period of time.

First, determine your budget allowance. Then take inventory of your closet. Assess items that need to be updated or replaced—for instance, a new tie or a new white blouse. To simply go shopping with nothing particular in mind usually costs you unnecessarily and fills your closet with mismatches.

Making wise purchases makes your money go further, and it also reveals good stewardship of your resources. Here are some important questions to ask when shopping:

1. What article in my closet will go with this item?

2. Is it of good quality? (Check seams, hems, lining, zippers, buttons, etc.)

3. Is this item on my "list of needs" or just an impulse purchase?

4. What type of care will it require—for example, dry cleaning or hand washing?

5. Will it need alterations? If so, can I afford them? (Alterations are usually worth the cost if they give a good article of clothing that perfect-fit look.)

6. How long will this be in style? Are the lines traditional or faddish? When you are tempted to buy clothes that will be out of style next season, perhaps you should consider buying only one, if it is otherwise appropriate.

7. How often can I wear this item in one season?

8. What is the exchange or refund policy of this store?

FORMAL ATTIRE

There comes a time in every person's life when only formal attire will do. Perhaps you are going to a prom, a ceremony, an awards banquet, or a formal holiday party. Because these occasions are rare, it is a good idea to go to a good rental shop for your needs. Buying a tuxedo that you may only wear once and will likely outgrow may not be a wise purchase. When an invitation says "Black Tie," that means a tuxedo for the guys and a floor-length formal gown for the girls. (The girls' invitation will have the same wording as the guys'). "Black Tie Optional" usually means that a dark business suit is appropriate for the guys, and a mid-calf (or "tea-length") dress that is of soft, elegant fabric is a good choice for the girls. If you are unsure what the expectations are for the event, ask a knowledgeable adult.

LESSON SEVEN

RSVPS AND THANK-YOU NOTES

CARING ENOUGH TO SEND YOUR VERY BEST

Learning Objective

To learn the proper mechanics for writing social correspondence.

Introduction

As a student, you probably enjoy all the advantages of the new technology emerging almost daily. You like e-mailing your friends, talking on your cell phone, and using your PDA (personal data assistant). Perhaps you are a blogger or have your own Web site. But there comes a time when only a personal, handwritten note will do.

Taking time to write a thank-you note, an invitation, a sympathy note, or a note of congratulations will do more to leave a favorable and lasting impression than you may realize, while making someone happy at the same time. All you need are the right tools and a little practice. Here are the things you need to keep handy in a convenient place: a good pen, postage stamps, an address book, and good paper with matching envelopes.

Writing notes can be fun. You just need to know when to write, what to say, and how to send them.

THE RIGHT TOOLS

It is always best to use nice paper or card stock and a pen with blue or black ink for writing. The most popular paper is fold-over paper that measures about 3 ½ x 5 inches after it is folded. You may begin writing at the top of the opened note or beneath the crease in the fold. (Beneath the crease is preferred.) Plain fold-over notepaper that does not have "Thank you" on the front has long been preferred over notebook paper. Appropriate writing papers include: plain, blank cards and small sheets of paper with no lines. Each of these must have a corresponding envelope.

> ## "Good manners are made up of petty sacrifices."
> —Ralph Waldo Emerson

REMEMBER THESE POINTS

- Answer an invitation within a few days of receiving it (or as soon as possible).

- Write a thank-you note within one week.

- Write the way you would speak to the person.

- Do not mention any dislike of the gift. (You can always thank the giver for thinking of you.)

- When you are acknowledging a gift of money, do not mention the amount but do say what you plan to buy with the money.

- Never begin a letter or note with an apology. You can express regrets later in the message.

- Read your note aloud for clarity and check all words for spelling.

- For thank-you notes, write simple sentences expressing your thanks for the gift or the kindness of the giver.

- Sign both your first and last name. The giver may know several Sarahs. You do not want the receiver to guess which one you are.

- A bread-and-butter note or a hospitality note is one you write when you have been an overnight guest or a weekend guest. This note is not very different from the thank-you note except the wording.

INVITATIONS AND REPLIES

The letters *RSVP* are often written or printed near the bottom of an invitation. They stand for *Répondez, s'il vous plaît.* The words are French, and they mean "Please respond." And they really mean you must give an answer.

If an invitation states "regrets only," it is necessary to reply only if you do not plan to attend. Remember, the host/hostess will definitely expect you at the appointed time if you do not answer the RSVP. If a phone number is given, you may telephone your answer; but if there is no phone number, you are expected to write your answer. A simple fold-over note is appropriate for this purpose.

THE USE OF TITLES

Titles are important, but once you learn a few rules, you will have no trouble:

- Females are addressed as Miss, Mrs., Ms., Dr., or other professional title. An unmarried woman uses "Miss" until she is about twenty-five. "Mrs." is used for married women and widows. "Ms." is used for single women and any time you do not know the status of the woman you are addressing. "Ms." is somewhat of a catch-all title; it is hardly ever a wrong choice.

- Until young men are college age, a title is not necessary before their name. A grown man is addressed with "Mr." or a professional title.

- Never use a title both before and after a name, such as, Dr. James Smith, M.D., or Ms. Mary Anderson, Esquire (a title used for attorneys). Exceptions include Jr., I, II, and III—they are part of a name and not really a title. You may correctly write: Mr. John Duncan Jr.

- Never sign your name with a title before your name, such as Mr. James Doolittle or Miss Amy Mosler.

ONE OF THE DEEPEST LONGINGS IN THE HUMAN SOUL IS TO BE APPRECIATED.

THE ENVELOPE

Write your return address on the top left corner on the face of the envelope, flush with the left margin. Social correspondence, including the envelope, should be handwritten, not generated on a computer printer. You may print, but never let your poor handwriting be an excuse for not writing.

Place a postage stamp on the envelope and place the handwritten note inside in such a way that when the receiver opens the envelope, he or she can pull the note out with the front side facing outward, ready to be opened from the bottom of the note. When you insert the note properly, and the recipient pulls it from the envelope, the fold will appear at the top.

The date goes on the inside of the note either in the top-right corner of the message or in the bottom-left corner at the end of the message.

Mary Beth Neal
123 Spring Garden Rd.
Franklin, KY 42134

Mr. and Mrs. Tom Williams
62 College St.
Franklin, KY 42134

EXAMPLES OF A THANK-YOU NOTE

The thank-you note has regrettably become something of a lost social grace in contemporary society. But you can show your good manners and demonstrate how much you care about others by making the small effort required to thank someone properly. E-mail messages, faxes, and phone calls are all very informal and are usually not appropriate for replacing a note of thanks. Say thank you in writing when you receive a gift or someone does you a special favor.

Here is an example of a simple thank-you note for a birthday gift:

Dear Mr. and Mrs. Williams,

You really know what I like. The latest DVD completes my set of that series. Thank you for such a perfect birthday gift.

Love,

Mary Beth Neal

June 6, 2007

CELL PHONES AND E-MAIL

CAN YOU HEAR ME NOW?

Learning Objective

To observe the proper use of phones, cell phones, and e-mail.

Introduction

Telecommunication skills are a must in the twenty-first century with new technology connecting us to more and more hardware and software that both ease and complicate our lives. We must remember that these eye-popping accessories are designed to connect us to individuals who still have very human feelings and perceptions.

In this chapter you will learn the proper way to make a personal and business phone call and how to send a proper e-mail message.

BASIC PHONE MANNERS

- *Always* identify yourself when you make a phone call.

- Smile when you say, "Hello." Believe it or not, people can hear the smile in your voice.

- If you're placing the call, ask the other person if this is a good time to talk. If it is not, ask when might be a convenient time for you to call back.

- Give the person on the other end of the line your undivided attention. Whether you are making or receiving the call, set aside whatever you're doing and focus on the conversation. Do not watch TV, play video games, surf the Internet, or engage in any other activity that may distract you from the call.

- Before you hang up, end the call on a positive and pleasant note and say good-bye.

- If you find you have dialed a wrong number, first confirm that you have reached the correct number by asking if you have reached 555-5555, and then apologize if you have reached the wrong number.

- When visiting someone else's home, always ask before using their phone for any reason.

TAKING A MESSAGE

Always be prepared to take a message when the phone rings. A pen and a message pad should be kept near each phone in the house for this very purpose.

When taking a message, be sure you take down in clear handwriting the following information: the person for whom the message is intended, the full name of the person who called, the time the call was received, a detailed description of the action being requested (for example, "Ask him to call me at 7:30."), and the phone number where the caller can be reached.

Here is a sample call:

"Hello." (smiling)

"Hi, Sue. This is Jeff. May I please speak to your brother, Matt?"

"I'm sorry, Jeff, but Matt just left to go to the store with Mom. Can I take a message?"

"Yes, ask Matt to call me when he gets home. I'm at my aunt's. The number here is 555-1212."

"I've got it." (Read back the message you have written down.) "'Jeff called at 7:00. He wants you to call him at his aunt's house. The number is 555-1212.' I'll give him the message."

"Thanks, Sue. Good-bye."

"Good-bye, Jeff."

> ## "MANNERS ARE THE HAPPY WAY OF DOING THINGS."
>
> ### —Ralph Waldo Emerson

LEAVING A VOICE MESSAGE

These days nearly every home and office phone is equipped with some form of voicemail or answering device, so be prepared to leave a clear and concise message with a machine. Here are the points of pertinent information that need to be included in your message:

- your full name

- the name of the person you are trying to reach

- the day and time of your call

- your telephone number, if you request a return call

- your message

- repeat your telephone number slowly

CELL PHONE COURTESY

A cellular phone can be a lifesaver in an emergency. It can also be a real nuisance to the people around you. According to one English research firm, 58 percent of the teens in the U.S. have cell phones, and 24 percent of the owners feel they have to answer a call, *no matter what.* Please let me assure you that the simple ringing of your cell phone does *not* mean you must answer it.

There are many places and occasions where it is simply inappropriate to take a call from anyone but a parent. When you are with friends at the mall or in a store and another friend calls to chat, you may excuse yourself for a moment to talk privately; however, it is polite to ask the friends who are with you, "Do you mind if I take this call?" (Wait for an answer.) Usually, you should ask the caller if you can call him or her back later.

Keep in mind that private conversations should not become public. No one wants to listen involuntarily to a one-sided conversation.

If you receive an important call while riding on public transportation, keep your voice down and make your conversation as short as possible.

Restaurants, churches, movie theaters, libraries, and classrooms are among the places where a cell phone should never be allowed to ring. Turn off your cell phone or set it to "vibrate" before an embarrassing situation arises, particularly when you are on a date or in a place where you know that talking on the phone will disturb others.

For safety, use a hands-free phone in your car if you must talk while driving. Never dial a number unless your car is stopped, and never look up a telephone number while the car is moving. Use your voicemail feature instead of answering the car phone, especially in heavy traffic or hazardous weather conditions.

E-MAIL AND NETIQUETTE

If you combine the words *net* and *etiquette*, you get *netiquette*, which describes the way people should behave on the Internet.

When writing an e-mail, you may think that the message is only between you and the person you are writing, but your e-mail is far from private. Once you hit that "send" button, your message is traveling unprotected through cyberspace where anyone with the know-how can pick it up. So consider your e-mail to be as public as a postcard or perhaps even a billboard. Let this be your guide as to what is and is not an appropriate e-mail. This is especially true when posting messages on a Web site. For many manners-related reasons—again, see the Golden Rule—never write *flame* messages containing personal insults or unnecessarily strong opinions.

Spam is a term that describes unwanted, irrelevant e-mail. The word comes from the name of a canned-meat product, which is a hodgepodge of different meat products pressed together. Not everyone likes it. The "forwards" that you receive and may enjoy can quickly become spam or junk mail if you forward them on to others. Overloading someone's in-box with unwelcome e-mail is bad manners.

Keep in mind that chain letters are illegal. And so is sending copyrighted material or another person's thoughts and ideas and calling them your own—also known as stealing.

EMOTICONS AND ACRONYMS

The little faces we create with letters and/or punctuation using the keyboard are often used as e-mail shorthand to express emotions and facial expressions. They are called "emoticons" and may be used in fun with close friends, but emoticons should not be used in business correspondence or in any kind of serious communication. The English language has at least half a million words we can use to say what we mean; leaning on cute little variations of smiley faces can encourage lazy thinking and writing.

Acronyms are formed by the first letters of a phrase or name containing several words, such as BBB (Better Business Bureau) and NFL (National Football League). Acronyms are often used among peers as "insider" language or as shorthand for words used repeatedly within a group, business, or organization. When sending messages over the Internet, it is imperative that you be clear in your communication. Using acronyms, abbreviations, and even slang can be confusing to your reader. If you are stumped trying to figure out someone's acronyms, there are free Web sites that offer "translations" for many of them. Such terms as LOL ("laugh out loud" or "lots of love") and BTW ("by the way") should not be used in business correspondence or other serious communication.

ACTIVITY

Write an e-mail and have it critiqued for the following points:

- Are the grammar and spelling correct?

- Is there jargon such as an acronym the recipient may not recognize?

- Does your subject line tell the recipient what to expect?

- Does your message begin positively or negatively?

- Are proper nouns and the first letter of sentences capitalized?

"Be kind. Everyone you meet
is fighting a hard battle."

—T. H. Thompson

LESSON NINE

THE PERFECT HOST AND THE WELCOME GUEST

Learning Objective

To be a gracious host by anticipating your guests' needs and planning for opportunities to entertain them. You will also learn how to be the perfect guest in someone's home.

Introduction

The secret to being a good host is to anticipate your guests' needs before they arrive. You can practice this by pretending you are a guest in your own home and applying the Golden Rule.

Being a host can be as much fun as being a guest if you anticipate the needs of your guest(s). One definition for *anticipate* is "to feel or realize beforehand" (Dictionary.com). Think of it this way: When you see that someone is tossing a ball to you, you hold out your hands in anticipation of catching it. Or perhaps when you were a small child, you put out cookies and milk on Christmas Eve because you were anticipating a visit from Santa Claus.

As a gracious host, you want to foresee *all* the needs of your guest(s). For instance, your guest will want to know what activities you have planned so that he or she may bring the appropriate clothing. Gracious hosts who prepare for and anticipate their guests' needs are well-remembered hosts.

PLAYING HOST

When your guests arrive, greet them at the door with a smile. Offer to take their coats, hats, luggage, and whatever they are carrying. Introduce your visiting friends to others in your home (if appropriate). Show your guests the location of the restroom as well as the bedroom where they will be staying so they can unpack when the time comes. Offer to supply anything they may have forgotten, such as a toothbrush or toothpaste.

If your friends have traveled some distance and it is not mealtime, offer them a snack and something to drink. (You will know what to offer them to eat and drink because you have already anticipated and inquired about any dietary restrictions. Do not ask the reason they do or do not eat certain foods.) Always serve your guests first, even snacks.

You will want to plan activities around the likes and preferences of your guests. Avoid anything that might make them uncomfortable. For instance, if you learn that a guest is afraid of heights, do not plan a trip to the tallest building in your city. If you discover such a dilemma after the guest arrives, always have a back-up plan.

While there are guests in your house, you should not make any plans that leave your guests out. Nor should you ask another member of your family to take over entertainment duties while you find something else to do. At all times, treat your guests the same way you would like to be treated.

Finally, cheerfully clean up after your guests leave.

MANNERS TRIVIA:
"In the Middle Ages only the nobility had special food knives, which they took with them when traveling: hosts were not usually expected to provide cutlery for guests."

—Margaret Visser, *The Rituals of Dinner*

WHEN YOU ARE A GUEST

The key to being a good guest means going along with the plans your hosts have made and being pleasant and agreeable under all circumstances. One of the goals for any guest is to be invited back again. Here are some guidelines to follow that will help you get a second invitation. If you accomplish these goals, you will surely be a welcome guest again and again.

- First, remember you are a guest. Do not take liberties you might feel free to take at home.

- As a first-time visitor, it's nice to bring the hostess a small gift such as food or flowers. Do not give the hostess personal items such as perfume, cologne, or bath powder.

- If you are spending the night, take along your personal toiletry articles so you will not have to borrow any.

- Be neat with your things. Do not scatter your clothing, personal items, or bath towels on the floor. Hang your towels on the rack. (You may be expected to use the same towel more than once.) Bring a plastic bag for your used clothing.

- Make your bed every morning.

- Be courteous, respectful, and quiet when others are quiet.

- Offer to help with everything from cleaning the table to carrying groceries. (Making one offer is sufficient; do not be a pest.)

- If you have allergies or phobias, discreetly mention these to your host in private.

- Keep your feet and shoes off the furniture and the bed.

- Ask before making a phone call. Unless there is an emergency, do not ask to make a long-distance call.

- If you need a snack for energy, it is all right to ask if you know it will be a while until mealtime.

- Be kind to any siblings your friend may have.

- If everyone appears to be busy, entertain yourself for a time or simply stay out of the way. Do not expect to be entertained every minute you are in the home.

- Respect others' privacy. Do not roam the house, open drawers, snoop in closets, or open the fridge unless invited to do so.

- When you pack to leave, use the list you prepared before you left home. Do not leave articles the host will have to mail to you.

- Before you leave, thank your host for inviting you. If possible, tell them you had a great time.

- Write a thank-you note to your host and leave it in a highly visible place or mail it within a few days of your visit.

> Dear Sarah,
>
> I just want to thank you for your hospitality this last week. I've had such a fun time visiting you and your family! I hope that you can come to visit me sometime soon.
>
> Samantha Boyers

HOW TO EAT

DINING AT HOME AND IN PUBLIC

Learning Objective

To develop confidence in all dining situations to enable you to be considerate of others and not focus on yourself, being afraid you will make a mistake.

Introduction

Have you ever been in a situation where you were confused about which fork to use at a meal? Don't worry. Almost everyone has, at one time or another, been a little unsure or even embarrassed while eating in front of others. It's true that your manners are never on display more than when you are eating. But if you will keep in mind a few simple rules, you will be able to eat at any table without fear of embarrassing yourself. Who knows? Maybe one day you'll dine at the White House.

> ## "The world was my oyster, but I used the wrong fork."
> ### —Oscar Wilde

FORMAL PLACE SETTING

You won't often see a formal place setting outside of a banquet hall or five-star restaurant. But more than likely, you will be confronted by this dizzying array of utensils a few times in the course of your life. Don't panic! It may look complicated, but it's really not.

Below is the proper way to set the table for a formal dinner. Try it at home this evening and amaze your mother.

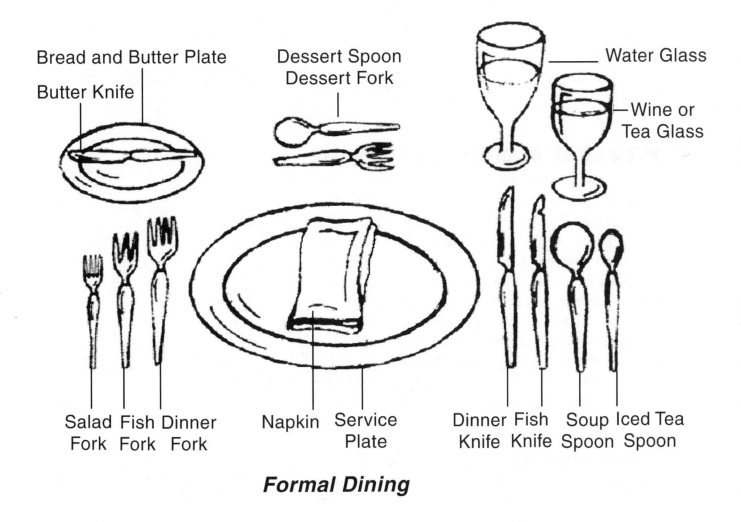

Formal Dining

Simple table setting:

- Placemat

- Dinner plate

- Napkin

- Glass

- Fork

- Knife

- Spoon

THE BASICS OF DINING IN THE HOME

Everyone comes to the table with hands washed and hats or caps removed. The gentlemen seat the ladies first by helping them with their chairs. When seated, no one should touch his or her beverage, silverware, or condiments, but wait quietly for the saying of the blessing. The hostess signals the beginning of the meal by placing her napkin in her lap, with fellow diners doing the same. (Guys, lay your napkin across one leg.) The host or hostess begins passing the food counter-clockwise, or to the right. But if someone begins passing the food to the left, do not say anything; simply continue passing it the same way. Pass each dish around the table one time. After that, pass a dish by the shortest route possible to the person who requested it, whether that is to the right or to the left.

Hold your spoon (and fork) as you would a pencil. If you drop a knife, fork, or spoon, ask politely for another one. If you pick it up, do not place it on the table. In a restaurant, leave it on the floor. If you drop your napkin, you may pick it up.

Use your napkin to dab your mouth (not swipe from corner to corner). Always use your napkin before drinking from a glass. Do not moisten a corner of your napkin and rub it on a soiled piece of clothing.

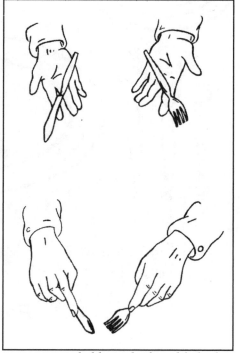

proper way to hold your knife and fork when preparing to cut something on your plate

Used by permission from Dorothea Johnson, founder and director of The Protocol School of Washington®

Excuse yourself to take care of the problem. Leave the napkin in your lap until you get up to leave the table. When you leave the table temporarily and when you leave for the last time, place the soiled napkin (unfolded) to the left of your plate or in your chair (not your plate).

To aid in everyone's good digestion, dinner conversation should always be pleasant. Do not talk about dieting, calories, your allergies, anything gory, or anything of an argumentative nature. Always say something nice to the person on either side of you.

Cut only one or two bites of meat at a time. When it's not in use, place your knife with the cutting edge toward you across the top of your plate. When the meal is finished, place your knife and fork securely across the upper part of your dinner plate. Watch for the host/hostess to signal the end of the meal by placing his or her soiled napkin on the table. Wait for the host/hostess to exit the dining table before you do. After rising, guys push their chairs (and their female partner's) back under the table.

HOW NOT TO EAT

- Never put your cloth napkin in your plate when you finish.

- Never slurp a beverage.

- Never scrape your plate or bowl with a piece of bread.

- Never shovel food into your mouth.

- Never talk with food in your mouth.

- Never take the last piece of food.

- Never take more than your share of the food in a dish (e.g., when there are four people and four pieces of meat).

- Never put used silverware on the table.

- Never put the utensil you are eating with in a community dish or platter.

- Never lick anything at the table.

- Never reach across the table or in front of someone to pick up anything. Ask someone to pass it.

- Never say "yuck" around food.

- Never smack your lips, burp, or pick at your teeth.

- Never leave a spoon handle protruding above the rim of a glass or cup. Place it on the saucer beneath it or prop the tip of the spoon on a plate.

- Never use a toothpick in public.

- Never eat with your elbows on the table. (It gives the appearance of sloppiness or of reclining on the table. However, as long as there is no food on a table, it is OK to prop an elbow while having a conversation.

DINING IN A NICE RESTAURANT

The same rules apply whether you are dining at a nice restaurant with family or on a date. When a guy and girl go to dinner in a restaurant, he offers to let her out at the door, then he parks the car. She waits just inside the restaurant door, and the two of them enter the dining area together. Once inside the restaurant, the girl follows the maitre d' or hostess to the table. Either the waiter or her date helps her with her chair. If the restaurant expects patrons to seat themselves, the guy leads the way to the table, while his date follows.

To stay within his budget, the guy may suggest something from the menu to his date. If he does not, the girl should ask him what he plans to order; then she chooses something in the same price range. If he does not tell her, she should choose something from the mid-price range on the menu.

If the order is less than perfect when it arrives, the guy politely asks the server to take care of it. For instance, the meat may not be cooked as you requested. If the girl excuses herself to go to the ladies' room, the guy stands when she leaves and when she returns.

When the meal is finished and you are ready to leave, ask the server to bring the check. When it comes, go over the figures to check for accuracy; if there is a mistake, quietly mention it to the waiter, who will take the check back to the cashier for correction. If you use a credit card, the waiter will fill in the subtotal and leave space for you to add a tip, fill in the total, and sign the credit slip. The waiter will give you one copy.

The customary tip is fifteen percent of the total bill before the tax is added. In very elegant restaurants, twenty percent is proper. Please note that some restaurants add the tip to your bill before presenting it to you; in this case, it is not necessary to tip twice. (The restaurant staff usually divides the tip among the server, the bus boy, and other helpers that you may not see.)

The guy helps the girl with her chair and her coat. Once outside, the girl waits for the guy to open the car door for her.

BUFFETS AND PARTIES

At a party or other social gathering, you may find yourself standing up and eating while balancing your food and drink. Here are some good manners you should use in that sometimes-awkward situation:

- Wait for the host/hostess to announce dinner before going near the food table.

- Watch the host/hostess and listen for instructions.

- Begin with the napkins and plates as you make your trip around or down the table, and place your napkin under your plate.

- Never appear to be eating from the buffet table or any serving dish. Wait until you leave the buffet table before putting anything in your mouth.

- Use the serving pieces or toothpicks provided and transfer the food from the serving table to your plate. (Keep the toothpick.)

- Never pick up something and then put it back on the serving dish.

- No double-dipping (i.e., taking a bite from a chip then using it to dip again).

- Never use your fingers or your own utensil to fish around the dip for a submerged chip or veggie.

- Do not heap your plate or stuff your mouth.

- Never spit anything out of your mouth. Use a paper napkin to take something out of your mouth, if you must. If the napkins are cloth, and you are expected to eat with your fingers, excuse yourself to the restroom to remove the offensive item.

- Do not place wet glasses or dishes on the furniture. Politely ask for a coaster or use a napkin.

- When you've finished eating, take your things to the place provided for used silverware, plates, and such.

- If you make a mess, apologize and offer to assist in the clean-up. Don't hide it.

"John Kennedy, Jr., his sister, and their mother were invited to the White House for dinner. John, Jr. was very young, and during dessert he spilled milk all over President Nixon's lap. The former president's son said, "He (President Nixon) didn't even blink. He just wiped it up, and I kind of just died slowly in the corner."

—Letittia Baldrige, Protocol Officer at the White House

FAST-FOOD DINING

These days, we eat at fast-food places more often than anywhere else outside the home. Even in such a relaxed, casual atmosphere, there are some good manners everyone should observe:

- Do not break in line.

- Be courteous to the order taker.

- Do not take more than your share of the condiments, such as napkins, straws, sugar, etc. In other words, do not be wasteful.

- Do not play with your food, straws, paper, plastic, etc. Do not make a mess.

- Maintain a low noise level within your group.

- When you've finished eating, clean up by taking disposable items to the trash.

- Guys, remove your cap or hat when entering any place that serves food.

- Never make a mess or play with the straws, sugar packets, and such on the table.

- The guy should refrain from cute antics; the girl will not likely be impressed. Girls should be neither too quiet nor full of empty chatter.

- At the counter, the girl orders first, or the guy can place the order for both of them. He helps her with her chair at the table, or the girl slides in first at a booth.

- The girl can get the guy's napkins, condiments, and such when she gets hers. He will probably be standing at the counter waiting for their order.

- The guy should take the initiative and take the trash to the receptacle when both have finished eating. Leave the table clean, or at least leave it uncluttered.

WHO PAYS?

If the guy and girl both have part-time jobs, and the parents do not object, the guy and the girl can share expenses, but the guy should generally take the most responsibility for paying. For instance, she might get the movie tickets ahead of time and let him buy the burgers before or afterwards. If the guy pays for their entertainment on most occasions, she should treat and pay now and then on a special occasion.

VITAL INFORMATION FOR EVERY SAVVY DINER, NO MATTER THE AGE

1. What should you do with empty packets of sweeteners?

Place your empty packet on the bread and butter plate or somewhere on your dinner plate, and prop the inverted iced teaspoon on the edge of your plate.

2. How to shift the fork after cutting meat and how to hold the fork American style for eating.

Shift the fork to your right hand and begin eating with the tines turned upward. When the meal is finished, place your knife and fork securely across the upper part of your dinner plate.

proper position for cutting meat

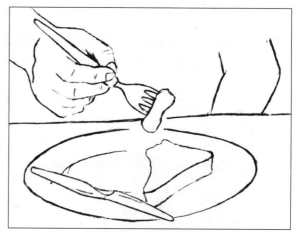

shifting the fork to your right hand

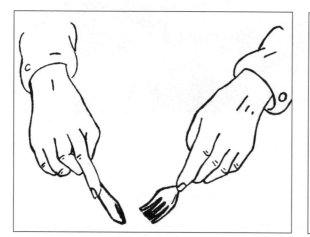

holding the utensils in each hand

proper position for utensils when meal is finished

Used by permission from Dorothea Johnson, founder and director of The Protocol School of Washington®

3. How to eat bread properly.

When the bread is passed, place your piece on the bread and butter plate, the salad plate, or your dinner plate. Pinch from a large roll and butter one bite at a time; then, place the knife across the top of the bread and butter plate. Biscuits should be halved, and a piece of cornbread may be eaten without breaking or pinching from it. (Reason? It crumbles.)

4. How do you eat properly if you are left-handed?

If you are left-handed, you are probably accustomed to living in a right-handed world. The table will be set the same way for both right and left-handed diners. Simply use the hand you are more comfortable using; it is better not to rearrange the place setting.

5. In order to avoid spills and accidents, what is the proper way to serve from the left and remove from the right (and the reason)?

Servers will serve food from your left and remove plates from your right.

Servers will serve beverages from your right. When food is passed family style, you may serve yourself before passing a dish to the person on your right. (Reason? It may be a long time before it comes back around to you.) Be ready to pick up a dish or platter that you see in front of you and pass it to the right after the host or hostess begins the process. Do the same with the condiments, which are substances, such as the salt and pepper, used to flavor or complement the food. (Never use salt or pepper before tasting your food. Reason? It is an insult to the chef.) (Note of interest to teens: Mr. J. C. Penney would not hire anyone who seasoned his or her food before tasting it.)

6. Diners should learn to pass the condiments or food in front of them to fellow diners.

If you need something such as the butter, ask someone to pass it to you. Say, "Please pass the butter." The person nearest the butter dish should pass it to you by the shorter route, right or left.

7. How to squeeze the lemon juice from a lemon wedge into your tea and what to do with it afterwards.

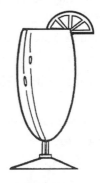

If you use lemon, hold it above your glass, and cover the wedge with your left hand while squeezing with your right hand, being careful not to squirt juice in someone's eye. Alternately, you may choose to drop the lemon wedge into the beverage and press it with the teaspoon.

8. What do you do with a wet iced teaspoon?

Place the wet spoon on the underlying plate or prop it on another plate with the tip of the handle resting on the table. You may also place the wet spoon on an empty sweetener packet.

9. How do you know which piece of silverware to eat with first and throughout the meal, and what do you do if you drop something such as your fork or your napkin?

Work from the outside of your silverware and move inward toward the plate as you go through the meal. For instance, if soup is the first course, pick up the soup spoon on the far right of the dinner plate. Hold your spoon like a pencil (as you also do your fork). If you drop a knife, fork, or spoon, ask politely for another one. If you pick it up, do not place it back on the table. In a restaurant, leave it on the floor. If you drop your napkin, you may pick it up.

less formal meal place setting

10. How to properly eat soup and what to do with the spoon when it is not in the diner's hand.

Soup may be served in a bowl or a cup. If it comes in a cup or a "tall" bowl, be sure to place your spoon on the plate underneath when you are resting or using your right hand for something else. (Reason? If you reach for your glass and the spoon handle is protruding upward, you might bump it and make a mess.)

11. What if you don't drink alcohol or other offered beverages?

You may refuse any beverage by simply saying, "No, thank you." No explanations are necessary. You can always drink water if alcoholic drinks are the only choice offered.

MANNERS TRIVIA:

The Anglo-Saxons used forks as early as the seventh century. But religious rulers said the utensils resembled the devil's pitchfork, and they disappeared for several hundred years. In 1633, King Charles I of England used a fork, and it's been much easier to eat steak ever since.

proper way to hold a fork

Parent/Teacher Pages

ETIQUETTE

MANNERS TRIVIA:

The word *etiquette* is French and means "ticket." During the reign of Louis XIV, a French lord or noble representing his province at the palace of Versailles was given a little "etiquette" to show where he was to stand in court.

HOW TO USE THIS BOOK
A WORD TO TEACHERS AND PARENTS

Dear Teacher or Parent:

This book is for you and the teens with whom you are entrusted. You have a rare opportunity to encourage, motivate, and challenge the next generation to practice The Golden Rule: "Do for others what you would like them to do for you." Good manners were God's idea, but The Golden Rule is for everyone. In fact, the *Wall Street Journal* cites this rule as the basis for all business and social interactions.

As students learn and, more important, practice good manners, self-consciousness will give way to self-confidence. Shy students should learn they are special because they are created in God's image, while bold, self-confident students should learn that they are dependent on others. But both shy and bold students must learn how important it is to think of others first.

Before delving into the parent/teacher pages, please read the student text first, as very little of the information has been repeated in the following pages. In the parent/teacher pages for each chapter you will find a teaching objective, preparation and supplies, and an explanation about the lesson, as well as instruction, critiques, and answers for the student pages. Whenever possible, emphasize student interaction and practice in each lesson.

Remember to challenge students never to use their newfound knowledge of manners to embarrass, criticize, or belittle the manners of another. Encourage your student(s) not to judge those who have had no opportunity to learn and practice proper rules of etiquette. Only when asked to in class should students critique one another's manners.

Manners Made Easy for Teens is merely an introduction to etiquette. For more detailed information about any specific area of etiquette, including formal dress and dining and interviewing for a job, please refer students to my books *Social Skills Survival Guide* (Broadman & Holman Publishers, 2003) and *The Etiquette Advantage* (Broadman & Holman Publishers, 1998).

LESSON ONE

MAKING A GOOD (FIRST AND LAST) IMPRESSION

Teaching Objective

To develop in students an awareness of how they are perceived by others and how to improve the impression they make by using the six S's to introduce themselves to others. You might tell your teen(s) about an embarrassing or awkward moment in your own life when you were a stranger at an event. Perhaps no one came over to introduce himself or herself to you, and you did not know how or even *if* you should introduce yourself. Tell your students that if you had learned the six S's earlier, you could have avoided this uncomfortable feeling.

Preparation and Supplies

A wall or hand mirror for demonstration and practice of facial expressions and body language.

About This Lesson

Life as a teen is not always easy. A teenager's body is growing from a child into a responsible adult, and sometimes our teens find themselves caught in between—no longer a child and yet not quite a grown-up. Your role as the instructor for this lesson is to gently and patiently encourage the teen while gladly applauding his or her efforts to learn and practice the six S's. One of your main goals is never to embarrass the teen.

ACTIVITY I

Go over the student pages with your teen(s), helping them to learn and memorize the six S's. Arrange for each student to have a partner with whom he or she can comfortably practice the six S's as well as proper body language postures. Create your own scenarios of meeting different types of people with different titles. Encourage the student(s) to think up different situations to practice in introducing themselves to new people. Keep a watchful eye on the practice sessions and monitor the tone, attitude, and method each partner uses when giving a critique of his or her partner. Make learning manners fun—see that no one gets embarrassed or gets their feelings hurt.

Tell the student(s) before the lesson that you will be stopping and correcting them in their practice sessions when you see a mistake, but that outside the classroom situation, you will not correct them in public because you do not want to embarrass them.

ACTIVITY II

Demonstrate various body language postures and ask the student(s) to tell you what they think about them. Re-create some negative messages you have seen people portray in their body language, such as, slumping, placing one's hands on the hips, standing with one's hands clasped in a *V* in front of the lower part of the body, and walking with one's hands in pockets. Always explain why the message is negative and try to give a positive alternative.

REVIEW

1. Why are first impressions so important? **Answer:** *Answers will vary.*

2. Name the six S's. **Answer:** *Stand, Smile, See their eyes, Shake hands, Say your name, Say the person's name back to them.*

3. Name at least three reasons we should always repeat someone's name when we are introduced. **Answer:** *1) It helps us remember it; 2) it assures that we say it correctly; and 3) people like it when we say their name.*

4. When is the only appropriate time to correct someone's manners? **Answer:** *In private, or when they ask us to do so.*

5. Why is it a good idea to give a little more information about yourself than simply your name? **Answer:** *To facilitate conversation.*

MAKING INTRODUCTIONS/ CONVERSATION

COMMUNICATING WITH EASE

Teaching Objective

To guide the student(s) into making easy conversation with a partner. You will also help them to comfortably and confidently make introductions that facilitate future friendships and conversations.

Supplies and Preparation

Lightweight balls, an egg timer (or anything that can silently keep track of the time spent in a dialogue or conversation), and a small bell or ringer of some kind to call an end to all practice conversations between partners. Suggested props for practicing introductions: hats/caps, a cardboard crown, white lab coat, a walking cane, a cowboy hat, or anything you have around that will help students identify the honored person when making introductions.

About This Lesson

After this lesson, your students will find it easier to make new friends and acquaintances and be prepared to converse comfortably with them.

First, they must learn to make a proper introduction. The purpose of an introduction is to make people known to one another by name and to make others feel welcome. When your students can exchange names and give descriptive information about each person, they will help others make small talk, making life more fun for everyone.

When it comes to talking, one student may be a smooth conversationalist, while another will hardly say a word unless you ask a direct question. Your job is to make conversation attractive to both personality types. Casual discussions should be enjoyable for both participants.

The "talker" may need help in listening, giving the partner a chance to say something. The "quiet one" may have trouble thinking of things to say, and you may have to form some sentences for him or her to demonstrate how to do it.

ACTIVITY FOR MAKING INTRODUCTIONS

Form a group of three persons to practice making introductions using different scenarios. One person will be the introducer and the other two will be introduced to one another. Then switch roles so that everyone gets a chance to practice making the introduction.

1. Go over the rules for introductions in the student pages.

2. Each student will practice with his or her assigned partners.

3. Analyze the practice session.

4. Review the rules again and help the students create some of their own introduction scenarios for further discussion or practice.

ACTIVITY FOR MAKING CONVERSATION

Discuss each bulleted point in the list with your student(s), making sure they fully understand the meaning. You may need to give brief examples or anecdotes to illustrate a point, or you may ask your student(s) to do so. If you are teaching a group and the students are comfortable with this idea, you may choose to have two people at a time come before the class to engage in a conversation. When time is up, the listening audience can offer comments or suggestions without making hurtful remarks.

Decide beforehand on a hand signal you can use to alert one partner who is talking too long before tossing the ball. If you have several conversational dialogues going at the same time, simply walk around the room and make notes of each group. Do not interrupt someone in mid-sentence, but if one partner is holding the ball too long, use your signal to alert him or her.

After a timed conversation, use your list of noted errors to instruct your students without embarrassing someone over a *faux pas* they might have made. Simply explain how some of the conversations you heard could have been better.

REVIEW

1. When is it acceptable to ignore introducing people? Why? **Answer:** *It is never acceptable to avoid introducing people simply because you cannot remember the rules or someone's name. Always make the effort.*

2. How do you decide who is the more important person when making an introduction? **Answer:** *Choose the older person, the female, or the person holding the more important position.*

3. Give an example of something you can say to a person when you cannot remember his or her name. **Answer:** *"I know we've met. Could you refresh my memory? I'm terrible with names." Or "Sorry, but I have simply gone blank."*

4. Why is it rude to interrupt, even if you know the correct answer or the right way to do something? **Answer:** *It is annoying to the speaker.*

5. Name some topics that are taboo for conversation around the dining table. **Answer:** *Dieting, gory things, argumentative subjects.*

6. How do you know if you are making "flattering" comments? **Answer:** *Your remarks will sound like exaggerated praise.*

7. Never laugh at others, only at _____ . **Answer:** *Yourself.*

8. (True or False) Accept compliments by saying "Thank you." **Answer:** *True.*

9. Give an example of an open-ended question. **Possible answer:** *"I had to leave early last night. How did the story end in the movie we were watching?"*

10. (True or False) Telling the truth does not mean you have to be brutally honest and hurt someone's feelings. You can always find something nice to say. **Answer:** *True.*

THE DATING GAME

A GUIDE TO GUY/GIRL SOCIAL INTERACTION

Teaching Objective

To give your student(s) much-needed knowledge about guy/girl relationships and to encourage them to grow in purity and maturity.

About This Lesson

As long as there are men and women, guy/girl social relationships will never go out of style. Teens need to know how to handle these situations, especially as they mature and interact more often with people outside their family.

Dating is much more complicated in modern times, even for teens from strong Christian homes with old-fashioned values. But the principles in this lesson should give both the parents and their teen(s) more confidence and self-assurance when navigating these waters.

Preparation

Arrange an opportunity for each student to interview an adult or a married couple whose relationship the teen admires and trusts. Or you may choose a widow or widower who would relish the idea of telling about the beautiful "romance" or "courtship" with the one they married. It is a good idea to assign the student(s) to adults who are not their parents, unless the parents prefer to be the interviewees for their own teen.

Ask several questions of the potential interviewees to ensure that their answers in an interview will be appropriate for your teen student(s). Purity before marriage for both the man and woman is very important, of course, but you will also want to choose couples who followed their parents' teachings and rules and who got their parents' permission before marrying when they were old enough. Most of us know a couple who eloped and enjoyed a long, happy marriage, but at the age of your young student(s), it is perhaps better not to encourage that idea.

TEACHING THIS CHAPTER

Most of this lesson is structured around sound, basic principles of social interaction. Engage your student(s) in open discussion about the various topics found in these pages. Tell the student(s) early in the lesson that you will assign them to an interview, and that they will later share what they learned from the interview.

The techniques used in this lesson are relatively easy to teach, but what you say as the instructor may make it one of the most important. Consider carefully the age and maturity of your student(s).

If you are teaching a number of students from different families, you may want to confer with those parents to learn their own family rules and guidelines concerning guy/girl social relationships.

THE INTERVIEW

Make a list of questions for the teen(s) to take to their interview. Some students may want to record their interview session. Here are some suggested questions for students to ask the couple or the individual in the interview:

1. How did you meet your mate?

2. Tell me about your fun activities together. What was the most memorable? Why?

3. How did you know you had found the mate God wanted for you?

4. What issues do you think a couple should agree on before they commit to one another for life?

5. Tell me about your wedding day.

6. I am _____ years old. What advice do you have for me?

After your students have conducted their interviews, reassemble the class, and discuss what they learned. Ask each teen to comment on his or her favorite part. Help the students write a thank-you note to the person or people they interviewed (see chapter 7).

LESSON FOUR
PUBLIC MANNERS

Teaching Objective

To teach the specific skills students need now as they mature into young adults—skills that will help them put the needs of others before their own and, at the same time, avoid embarrassment.

Preparation and Supplies

Arrange for a chair and table where a young man can seat a lady. Elevators, stairs, and escalators are also skills to teach. Perhaps you can arrange for an outing or field trip where these facilities are available.

About This Lesson

The purpose of this lesson is to enable your students to become more aware of how others perceive their behavior and how their actions affect others in public places. Teens are more easily embarrassed than younger students because they are in a transition period. Becoming equipped with the skills in this chapter will help them avoid being uncomfortable and self-conscious in new situations. Discuss the introduction to the student lesson with your student(s).

REASONS FOR THE RULES

In this lesson, you have been given answers for the section "Reasons for the Rules" that the students do not have. Spend some time giving the student(s) a chance to say what they think the reason is for each rule in the list.

For the remainder of the lesson, you can simply read along with the students, answering their questions and adding your own suggestions, which you may want them to write down.

1. It used to be that a man walked on the curbside of the sidewalk when walking with a lady to protect her from splashes of mud thrown up by carriage or wagon wheels. Paved roads have eliminated the need for such protection, but men should continue to walk on the street side. One exception might be when he needs to protect a lady from muggers and purse snatchers lurking in doorways. Then he walks on the inside. He simply uses his common sense to decide.

2. A guy extends his arm bent at the elbow so that the girl can hold on to him if she trips. If he simply puts his hand on her arm, he cannot prevent a fall.

3. When a door opens toward you, the other person is free to walk through the doorway.

4. With a push door, the guy is in the way if he tries to open it and let the girl go through before him. She must then squeeze by him and the half-opened door.

5. Elevators, no explanation needed.

6. Elevators, no explanation needed.

7. A guy's partner is usually on his right. Originally, chairs were very, very heavy, but even today, it is a nice gesture for a guy to help the ladies with their chairs.

8. Guys need to climb stairs and escalators behind the girl in case she falls.

9. This is simply a way of showing respect. Ask the student(s) to name other times they can think of when a hat or cap should be removed.

10. The guy always goes first any time there is an element of danger or the unknown. Movie theaters are not usually dangerous places today, but the tradition lives.

11. No explanation needed.

ENTERTAINMENT COURTESIES

Read over these points with the students, explaining when necessary. Remind the student(s) that a good way to prevent embarrassing yourself during a formal concert performance is to follow the cue of others. If possible, arrange to take your student(s) to a performance by a local symphony or ballet. Their lives will be enriched.

GOOD MANNERS WITH THE DISABLED

The word *handicapped* goes back in English history to when the British crown gave licenses and special caps to disabled veterans of war so they could beg on the street for a living. That's one reason the term is considered negative by persons with a disability. Read and discuss the five rules with your students. Discuss pages 28 and 29.

GOOD MANNERS WITH RUDE PEOPLE

A good reminder for your students is this quote from F. Scott Fitzgerald in *The Great Gatsby:*

> "Whenever you feel like criticizing anyone . . . just remember that all the people in this world haven't had the advantages that you've had."

LESSON FIVE

THE JOB INTERVIEW

Teaching Objective

To fully equip the student to pursue future employment.

Preparation and Supplies

Desk or table, chairs, classified ads, telephone, paper and pen, or word processing software. You will also need a blank job application form, which may be obtained from just about any local business. You will take your student(s) through the steps of applying for an imaginary hourly wage job, such as a sales position at a bookstore or fast-food restaurant. Choose the name of a real business in your area so that the student(s) can do some research on the company to prepare for a mock interview.

About This Lesson

Whether your students are entering the fast-food industry or applying for a sales job, they need the experiences of this lesson. The activities in this chapter will benefit them for a lifetime.

FIVE WAYS TO GET AN APPOINTMENT FOR AN INTERVIEW

1. *Ask an acquaintance of your parents, a teacher, or a church official* to introduce and recommend you.

2. Call for an *appointment* for an interview.

3. Contact the personnel office and pick up *an application.*

4. Send a *résumé* with a *cover letter.*

5. Apply online. Make certain that all necessary *information* is clearly included at the top of the page. Your application may be scanned and valuable information may not print near the top or bottom of the paper.

APPLICATION FORMS

Pick up a blank job application from a local employer or at an office supply store. Have the student(s) practice filling out the application. Be prepared to offer suggestions for the skills each student might have. Remind the student(s) of paid jobs they may have performed in the past: babysitting, washing cars, gardening, shoveling snow, cleaning gutters, caring for animals, mowing lawns, delivering newspapers, or counseling at a camp.

THE INTERVIEW

Before the mock interview, ask students to write down the date, time, and location of the interview (with directions). Instruct students to write the name of the company, the employer/supervisor, and the interviewer's name (if different from employer). Students should go to the company's Web site or to the library to learn about the company. They should talk to people who work there.

If you are teaching multiple students, role-play in groups of three or more people. One person will be the applicant, a second plays the receptionist, and a third plays the interviewer. The remainder of the group will act as spectators who listen and write down suggestions for improvement on the part of the applicant. During the role-playing activity, any of the participants may call time out to think or decide on the next course of action.

Instructor to student(s): "You have finally landed a sit-down interview with the human resource person where you are seeking a job. You have written down all the pertinent information such as date, time, location, and directions. You know the manager's name, the interviewer's name, and something about the various departments in the store. You have checked out the store's Web site several times.

"An interview provides an opportunity for the company and you, the job applicant, to exchange information so you can both decide whether this job is a good fit for you and the company.

"While you want to represent yourself in the best possible light every time, remember that each interview should be a learning experience.

"A résumé or application will sell your qualifications on paper, but in the interview you must sell *yourself* by the way you look, react, and conduct yourself. You are not expected to know everything, but your interviewer will be rating you on these points:

- The way you look—your grooming, your facial expressions, your clothes, and even your posture.

- The way you speak—your tone of voice, your enunciation (don't mumble), and your grammar.

- The way you answer questions—honestly or in exaggerated terms.

- Your intelligence is revealed in your alertness, your questions, your answers, and your overall attitude.

- Your determination comes through in your willingness to work and take on responsibility, your self-confidence, and even your cheerfulness.

- The way you discuss your former employer shows your loyalty or lack of it. Don't bad-mouth anyone. It only makes you look small.

- Your friendliness, enthusiasm, and tact are all part of your personality, which is an important qualification.

"Your feelings during the interview may range from being too self-assured to being scared out of your mind. To avoid both of these extremes, remember that you have something to offer, a real contribution, and you are not asking for charity; you are willing to work. The interviewer has been in your shoes before and knows how you feel. At the same time, don't act as though you are doing the company a favor by simply applying for the job."

PREPARING FOR THE MOCK INTERVIEW

The spectators should be given the instructions below for both the interviewer and the applicant. They will critique the behavior of the applicant; however, in rendering their assessment, they will mention first the applicant's strong points and the positive aspects of his or her performance before offering advice.

The Interviewer

You are in charge of hiring new personnel for the company. You have a staff of seven and one part-time worker who is leaving to attend college in another city. You prefer someone with sales experience who can be trusted to handle money. You are looking for someone with a good work ethic who has a congenial personality with whom you and the other employees can work comfortably. You need someone with initiative and a pleasant attitude.

The Applicant

After calling in response to the ad in the newspaper, you have been given an appointment time for an interview with the human resources manager. You have memorized the high points of your application or résumé and have prepared some intelligent questions to ask if you are given the opportunity.

THE INTERVIEW STEP-BY-STEP

Instructor to students: "The interview actually begins when you step out of your car. Someone may be watching from an office window to see how you handle yourself. Walk as though you know where you are going and hold your head up. When you reach the reception area, announce yourself clearly. Don't mumble your name."

Ask the student(s) to write out some questions and answers they might ask using the examples numbered 12, 13, and 14 on page 34 of the student pages.

Keep in mind that the script provided is only a model. You may write your own script for the interview.

CRITIQUING THE APPLICANT

Rate the student's performance using the following checklist as a guide. Add anything you see that might be helpful.

- Showed punctuality
- Confidently greeted receptionist
- Clearly stated name and purpose
- Appeared well groomed
- Was attired properly
- Was alert, interested
- Showed enthusiasm
- Allowed the interviewer to be in charge
- Used proper body language (no fidgeting)
- Spoke in a strong (not loud) tone of voice
- Showed responsiveness
- Made good eye contact
- Politely used words such as *please, thank you, excuse me*, etc.
- Gave a firm handshake
- Answered questions sufficiently
- Did not look at his or her watch
- Did not talk too much
- Did not ask about breaks and vacation time
- Did not ask about salary too early in the interview

WHAT TO WEAR

Teaching Objective

To help students make wise and mature choices about their attire for college interviews, job interviews, church functions, dates, etc.

About This Lesson

John Molloy, the famous *Dress for Success* author, says that "improper dress (attire) is the most common reason job candidates are eliminated." Most students today need all the help they can get because, unfortunately, people they meet will often judge their abilities, their intelligence, and their character by the way they dress. In this lesson, you will have the opportunity to help your teen(s) learn how to make the right choices to enhance their personal appearance. Proper manners and proper dress go hand in hand.

You will want to remind your student(s) that simply because a type of clothing is sold in a store does not mean that is always appropriate. Fashions come and go, but good taste is always in style. Help your students to be informed, discriminating shoppers.

ACTIVITY

1. Assign your student(s) a trip to their closet, after which they will return to class with their choice of clothes of what they would wear to a job or college entrance interview.

2. Make arrangements for a field trip to an upscale department or specialty store and also to a shop that sells formal wear. Explain to the manager or salesclerk that you are studying about proper dress and ask him or her to take time to show your student(s) how to select quality apparel.

Go over the chapter with your student(s), explaining and discussing points when necessary to ensure clarity and understanding. You may have several good tips of your own to add to the information presented here.

Ask your student(s) to bring items they choose from their closet and evaluate their selection(s) as a class, or provide a private student consultation for each one.

LESSON SEVEN

RSVPS AND THANK-YOU NOTES

Teaching Objective

To help your students become proficient in writing social correspondence and enjoy doing it.

Supplies and Preparation

Plain paper, pencils, and pens with blue or black ink. Ask the students to purchase a box of plain notes with corresponding envelopes. If your class is small, you may decide to purchase a box and provide two to each student to use after they have practiced.

Suggest to parents that they give their student a gift of nice stationery, or suggest to your students that they ask for nice stationery for their birthday or Christmas that can be used later. Many mail-order stationery providers offer very nice notepaper with the buyer's name and address.

While this lesson recommends that blue or black ink be used for serious social correspondence, your students may enjoy using other colors, stickers, and such for fun, informal, even playful notes. But for the purposes of this lesson, begin by teaching the more formal approach.

About This Lesson

This lesson should be fun for the instructor and student. Written correspondence will never go out of favor, no matter the advances in technology, because it is exciting to receive a personal, handwritten note or an invitation in the mail. (We have so much unwanted mail sent to our mailboxes addressed to "Occupant.") With your student(s), read and discuss the material in the student pages.

MAKING A THANK-YOU NOTE

Using plain printer paper, cut a sheet in half horizontally. Now rotate each of the two pieces so that they are longer from top to bottom. Then fold each of the halves in the middle, and you will have two fold-over notes for practice. Have the student(s) make several of these. They may practice with pencils and erasures until they get their note "just right."

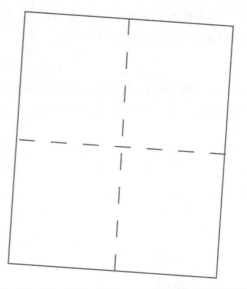

PRACTICE WRITING A NOTE AND ADDRESSING AN ENVELOPE

After practicing, have the students write a note and address the corresponding envelope to thank their parents (for anything) and place it on a parent's bed pillow, the kitchen table, or some other easily seen place in the home.

Also, ask students to write a thank-you note to the person(s) they interviewed in chapter 3.

Remind the student(s) of the comma after the salutation and after the closing. There should be a one-line space between the salutation and the body of the note, another one-line space between the body and the closing.

LESSON EIGHT
CELL PHONES AND E-MAIL

Teaching Objectives

To facilitate practicing and learning the proper use of phones, cell phones, e-mail, and portable electronic devices.

About This Lesson

Good telecommunication skills are a must in today's world with new technology connecting us to more and more hardware, software, and digital devices that both ease and complicate our lives. We must remember that these accessories are designed to connect us to individuals who have feelings and perceptions.

Students today must be proficient in the non-offensive use of cell phones, e-mail, voice mail, instant messaging, and a myriad of other devices, as well as in the effective, business-like use of them. In this chapter, the student(s) will make a personal telephone call and send a proper e-mail message under the critical eye of you, the instructor.

Teach the information in the student pages and then focus on role-playing activities.

Useful Supplies

A mirror, pencil and pad, a phone, and use of the Internet.

MAKING A PROPER TELEPHONE CALL

Practice making proper telephone calls by role-playing the dialogue in the student pages. Here are some points of critique to keep in mind:

1. Did the caller identify himself with first and last names?

2. Did the caller speak to you by name and ask if he had reached 555-5555?

3. Did the caller say "please" when he asked to speak to a particular person?

4. Was the caller waiting quietly and not making noise when you or the requested individual returned to the phone?

5. Did the caller ask if this was a convenient time to talk?

6. Was the caller chewing gum, eating, or drinking while on the phone?

7. Did the caller keep the call brief?

8. Before the caller ended the call, did they say good-bye after first asking if you had any questions or comments before you hang up?

9. Did the caller say something nice before saying good-bye (such as "I'll see you tomorrow at school")?

Now ask the students to role play making a call to a wrong number. Critique the call based on the following:

1. Did the caller say, "Have I reached 555-0000?"

2. Did the caller apologize for the error?

ANSWERING A PHONE PROPERLY

Ask the caller to critique the individual who answered the phone based on the following points:

1. Could you hear a smile and pleasant tone when the individual said hello?

2. If the caller does not identify himself should the answerer say, "May I ask who is calling?" or "Who is this?"

3. Did the answerer ask if you could wait for the requested person to come to the phone?

4. Did the answerer quietly lay down the receiver in order to find the requested person?

5. Did the answerer leave the phone to get the person, or did he/she just shout out the name?

6. If the requested person was unavailable, did the answerer ask to take a message?

7. Did the answerer write down the message?

8. Did the message include a name, date, and return phone number?

WRITING AN E-MAIL

Ask the student(s) to write an e-mail and critique it for the following points:

• Are the grammar and spelling correct?

• Is there jargon such as an acronym the recipient may not recognize?

• Does your subject line tell the recipient what to expect?

• Does your message begin positively or negatively?

• Are proper nouns and the first letter of sentences capitalized?

LESSON NINE

THE PERFECT HOST AND THE WELCOME GUEST

Teaching Objective

To nurture a desire in students to be happy, well-mannered guests and well-remembered hosts.

About This Lesson

Nearly everyone will perform the duties of a host as well as being an invited guest sometime in life. Yet many people fear the idea of being either or both. After this lesson, your students will be armed, prepared, and looking forward to the opportunity.

TEACHING SUGGESTIONS

- Review the material in the student pages and ask for questions and comments.

- Plan a scavenger hunt in which you ask your student(s) to find items a guest might look for in an unfamiliar house. Parents and family may help with this activity. Consider assigning a couple of planned sleepovers so the student can practice being a guest and also being a host.

- Teach the students to anticipate (to decide ahead of time) where their guest will hang or place his or her things and where the bath linens and soaps are stored. Remind them to point out to their guest anything in the home that might be a little unusual to visitors. For instance, the handle on the shower may be difficult to find, see, or turn. Perhaps the hot and cold water spigots are backwards. Always try to anticipate any problem or dilemma your guest might encounter.

- Ask each student to make a list of items and services in his or her house that a guest might need help in finding. Remind the student(s) that the list should be compiled with the needs of the guest and the length of their stay in mind. See suggested list on page 95.

- Remind your student(s) that a host should always tell the guest to please ask for anything he or she may have forgotten to bring. It is also a good idea to ask if the guest has any allergies.

- An appropriate space for their suitcase

- Closet space for hanging clothes

- Drawer space for folded clothes

- Fresh flowers are an especially nice touch

- Alarm clock

- Tissues

- Hand lotion

- Bottled water

- Scented candle (if your guests are not allergic)

- Basket of small snacks such as peanuts, mints, and fresh fruit

- Extra blanket

- Allergy-free pillows

- Small fan

- Bathrobe

- Bath linens

- Counter space or personal drawer in the bathroom

- Personal items, such as a hairdryer

- Bedside lamp for reading

- Selection of books of general interest and a Bible

- Pen, paper, stamps, and writing table or lapboard

- Small night light for safe trips to the bathroom

BEING A GUEST

Help students make a list of personal items each of them will need to pack for a trip or an overnight stay. Some articles will be common among the students, and some will be unique to each student, such as medication or their contact lens cleaner and case.

LESSON TEN

HOW TO EAT

DINING AT HOME AND IN PUBLIC

Teaching Objective

To help students become comfortable and confident in all dining situations.

Preparation and Supplies

Photocopy and laminate the formal place setting illustration as well as the simple table setting illustration without the labels that are founded on the next couple pages. Cut out the pieces and later ask the student(s) to arrange the place setting without looking at the labeled illustrations, if possible. For practice, provide these paper or plastic table implements: service plates (any plate larger than the dinner plate), dinner plates, salad plates*, bread-and-butter plates, dessert plates*, bread-and-butter knifes, dinner forks, dinner knives, soup spoons, iced teaspoons, dessert forks, dessert spoons, which may be the same as the salad plate and place spoons, water glasses, iced tea glasses, soup bowls, plates for soup bowl (any plate large enough for the bowl), platters or bowls for passing, and paper or cloth napkins.

* The same size and shape plates may be used.

About This Lesson

With the delicious possibilities for hands-on experiences in this lesson, you and your student(s) should enjoy practicing good table manners. Areas covered in this chapter include family dining, restaurants, and fast-food dining, as well as buffets and parties, where you often stand while you eat.

ACTIVITIES

Here are a few suggestions for dining-related activities to try with your student(s):

- Practice setting a formal and informal table.

- Practice holding the knife and fork properly. See text and illustrations in the *Social Skills Survival Guide* for additional guidance.

- Encourage the student(s) to host a small dinner party at home.

- Arrange an in-home meal or take your class to an upscale restaurant. Choose a restaurant you can work with to provide the meal and the service you need to teach this lesson. Enjoy!

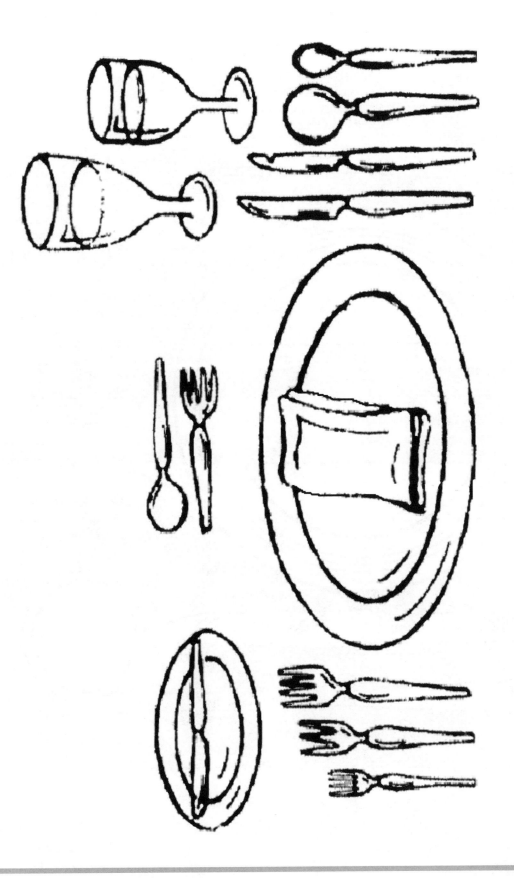

NOTES